We are only as successful as the dreams we dare to live,
the challenges we are prepared to face, and the sacrifices
we are willing to make. We can see our challenges as
opportunities, or we can see them as obstacles.

We can see them as a reason to succeed or as an excuse to fail.

The choices we make today will
ultimately determine our future tomorrow.

Praise for
Success Is Not a Spectator Sport

Ready to change your life? Then dive into Charles Marcus' book for a plan with immediate, positive results. With his 'You CAN do it' approach, he shows you exactly how to invite more friendship and opportunity into your life. Even the procrastinators will find themselves acting to transform their lives and thanking Charles Marcus for partnering with them to make it happen.
  Kare Anderson, author of *Getting What You Want,*
  Beauty Inside Out and *Resolving Conflict Sooner*

Success Is Not a Spectator Sport *is a magnificent, comprehensive step-by-step guide that shows you precisely how to achieve success in all areas of your life. Don't miss this opportunity to learn from Charles Marcus, an expert who "walks his talk" and gives you the information and inspiration you'll need to develop your potential. This book will take years, if not decades, off your learning curve!*
  Jeff Keller author of *Attitude Is Everything*

I'm not sure if it's possible to compile all of the world's greatest success strategies into one single volume, but with Success Is Not a Spectator Sport, *Charles Marcus comes close. This profound yet easy-to-read book will move you off the bench and onto the starting line-up in the winning team of life.*
  Joe Tye, author of *Your Dreams Are Too Small*

So often we sit on life's sidelines and miss the best part of the game. Charles Marcus has provided a valuable tool—pick it up NOW—put it to work NOW. Get off the bench and back in the game NOW.
  W Mitchel, CPAE, author of *It's Not What Happens to You, It's What You Do About It*

Charles Marcus delivers more than just a "FEEL GOOD" message in this book. He gives you an action plan for you to have the life you want to live. If you've heard Charles speak, you know that this action plan isn't just words, he's living proof that the program works.... I recommend that people read this book...and take appropriate action.

Jonathan T. Weaver, Principal, Peak Performers Network

Charles Marcus is living proof where there is a will there is a way. As you read this book you will feel everything is possible...for you!

Patricia Fripp, CSP, CPAE, past president National Speakers Association and author of *Get What You Want and Make it! So You Don't Have to Fake It.*

I'm a firm believer in the strategic approach to life and career that you espouse. You have laid out in a concise logical format the essential elements of achieving success defined in the "Reader's" terms. Your pathway to success can apply to any walk of life. Often times in other readings, we are left with ideological statements of "Winning Ways" that do not provide you with sufficient insights into the heart of the subject matter. This is certainly not the case with Success Is Not a Spectator Sport. *You have spelled out in a very clear and detailed fashion the step by step processes that you and others have followed to achieve success in both your professional careers and personal lives. Your work will serve as an invaluable guide for all of your readers.*

Robert M. (Bob) Bissett, Senior Vice-President
Toronto Centre District, Personal and Commercial Client Group
BMO Bank of Montreal

After reading Charles Marcus' book, you will truly understand how the decision to take action in life is the one most critical to success. Charles hits the nail on the head in Success Is Not a Spectator Sport!

Bob Urichuck, international speaker and author of
Online for Life: The 12 Disciplines for Living Your Dreams

Charles' book is a gem. He models leadership and success by openly sharing with us his story. He gives us practical assessments, tough questions, and how-to points. He provides inspiring examples that knock out many of our own excuses. This is all delivered in a readable, entertaining writing style that feels like a coaching conversation with someone who has lived his own advice. This is a must-read for anyone wanting to increase their success and happiness.

Jim Clemmer, expert on Practical Leadership and
author of five international bestsellers, including
Pathways to Performance, Growing the Distance
and *The Leader's Digest*

To succeed in life you have to play the game. You cannot sit on the sideline.
Success Is Not a Spectator Sport *shows you how to do that. If you want to move up the success ladder, implement the suggestions given in this book.*

Azim Jamal, author of the *Corporate Sufi* and the
national bestseller *7 Steps to Lasting Happiness*

For anyone who has ever thought that success in living their dreams was only for other people, this book is for you. Charles Marcus offers up a comprehensive, step-by-step how-to-plan to refocus your thinking, attitude and your efforts into a laser beam of action, that if applied, can ONLY result in your dreams becoming your reality!

Janet Matthews, Canadian co-author of
Chicken Soup for the Canadian Soul

If you are looking to crystallize your thinking and simplify your approach to success, then this book is for you! It will show you exactly what to do in order to have more and become more in the process. The questions asked and exercises given are what you need to change your life!

Larry Winget, speaker and author of
Shut Up, Stop Whining and Get a Life

success

is not a
spectator
sport

How to Take
Action and
Achieve More

Charles M. Marcus

Published by Creative Bound International Inc.
on behalf of
The Empowerment International Group
5863 Leslie Street, Suite 312
Toronto, Ontario M2H 1J8
Canada

ISBN 1-894439-14-7
Printed and bound in Canada

The author and publisher have made every attempt to locate and acknowledge copyright holders of quoted material. If we have inadvertently made any errors or omissions, kindly inform us so that we may correct any future reprints and editions. Thank you.

Text editor: Carol Clarke
Production by Creative Bound International Inc. 1-800-287-8610
        Book design by Wendelina O'Keefe
        Cover image © Getty Images

National Library of Canada Cataloguing in Publication

Marcus, Charles M. (Charles Michael), 1952-
        Success is not a spectator sport : how to take action and achieve more / Charles M. Marcus.

Co-published by Empowerment International Group.
ISBN 1-894439-14-7

    1. Success. 2. Goal (Psychology) I. Empowerment International Group. II. Title.

BF637.S8M358 2004   158.1   C2004-900587-1

I dedicate this book
to my wonderful and supportive wife Mary—
I could not have done this without you—
and to my very special children,
Daniel and Rachel,
who are the joy of my life.

I love you all very much.

Acknowledgments

Success is not a spectator sport, nor is it a solitary sport. This book would not have been possible without so many people who have contributed to my success in so many ways: Vidal Sassoon who gave me a chance when many others wouldn't, and who taught me so much about leadership, service and values; Andrew Bell whose discipline and philosophy gave me back my ability to speak, and taught me about self-esteem and courage; and Joseph Scaglione who took a risk on a novice salesperson from Manchester, and taught me so much about building relationships and the art of selling. Each of these individuals seemed to come in to my life at the right time and for all the right reasons.

There are also many people I have worked with and met in my travels over the years, people who have inspired me by a book I have read or a seminar I have attended and whose wisdom and experience are reflected in these pages.

I want to thank *Toastmasters International* and all the incredible people I have met through that organization over the years, and my friends at *Rotary International* for giving me the opportunity to speak at so many of their clubs and conventions when I was first starting out and building my speaking business.

I would probably have not written this book or be where I am today in the speaking business if it were not for my colleagues at the *Canadian Association of Professional Speakers*, the *National Speakers Association* and the *International Federation for Professional Speakers*. So many of you have inspired and encouraged me to write this book and believed in me from 'day one' in my dream and goal to become a professional speaker. You know who you are. Thank you from the bottom of my heart. You guys are the best.

Thank you to my editor, Carol Clarke, for your advice, support and expertise. You have been a pleasure to work with, and first class in every way. Also a big thank you to Gail Baird, Wendy O'Keefe and all the team at Creative Bound International. You have made an outstanding contribution to this book. I look forward to working with you on future projects.

Of course, I would also like to thank my clients in the speaking business and customers from my sales and hairdressing days. You taught me the discipline of perseverance and the value of excellence that you will read about in these pages.

Success is about constantly learning and being open to learn. Over the last few years, I have been honored to be able to speak to many organizations around the world, to work with some truly visionary leaders, to meet outstanding people, and to learn so much from them. I thank them for that experience. Hopefully, I can give something back.

Last, but not least, I would like to thank you, the reader, for honoring me by reading this book. You are so important to me.

To your success and your own journey,
Charles M. Marcus

Contents

Introduction

Over the years I have been blessed with much success. This is a bold state-ment, but I say it with confidence. However, on the way across each 'step-ping stone' of success, I have had to experience failure, setback, challenge and defeat. Because of my struggles, I have come to realize that success is really formed during the journey itself.

Success is largely dependent on the definition and rules you create for it. It grows and flourishes by your terms, not by the measurements or opinions of others. Once defined and set into action, though, it's important that you stick to your goals. To that end, this book was created to inspire and sup-port the fulfillment of your dreams.

Success Is Not a Spectator Sport has been a long time in the making. Within these pages I have tried to share with you my experiences, both good and bad, and offer you the best and most significant lessons I've learned over the years. I have tried to write as I would speak to you—in the only way I know—honestly, and from the heart.

It is my fervent hope that some ideas from this book will resonate with you and that you will be motivated to apply them in your own life. Please use this book as your ongoing resource guide: keep coming back to it, redo the exercises, re-think them, highlight the sections that are important to you alone. It will serve you well.

Get in the Game

Remind yourself regularly that you are BETTER than you think you are. Successful people are not superhuman. Success does not require a super intellect. Nor is there anything mystical about success, and success is not based on luck. Successful people are just ordinary folks who have developed a belief in themselves and what they do. Never sell yourself short.
— David J. Schwartz, author of *The Magic of Thinking Big*

What Does Success Mean to You?

I take success very seriously. It is something I am passionate about and constantly striving for. As I was preparing to write this book and contemplating the topic, I came to two conclusions. First, that success means different things to each of us. Second, that it should be constantly evolving. Therefore, the first step in your journey to success is to check your personal compass and determine your direction.

To many, success seems elusive and personally challenging. They are looking for a magic formula to unlock the secret of why some are so successful and why others are not. In the course of this book, you will find out how to achieve all the success you desire in your life, both personally and profes-sionally; however, before you can take that first step, you need to identify, examine and define what success means to you. Does it mean having mate-rial wealth or possessions; admiration from your peers; fame; the satisfac-tion of being a great parent; or helping others less fortunate than yourself? Maybe it is all of the above, some of the above, even none of the above.

Only you can identify the answer for yourself. Only you know what drives your passions and obsessions. What is it that will give you that sense of sat-isfaction that you so much want to achieve? Take a few minutes now to complete the following exercise. It will help you narrow down what success means for you.

Exercise: A success story

Think about a time that you completed a project or task that made you feel particularly 'on your game.'

A: Describe the situation.

_____

_____

_____

_____

_____

B: What was it about the situation that gave you so much satisfaction?
   (What specific actions or feelings contributed to the situation?)

_____

_____

_____

_____

_____

Note: You may want to do this simple exercise a couple of times as you work through your definition of success.

Exercise: Defining success for you

Using the situation(s) you described in the previous exercise, try to determine the elements that you think define success for you.

For example: When I asked a colleague the questions from the previous exercise, she related her experience as a member of the design team for a sales workshop. As it was very well received, the workshop was subsequently rolled out across the country for both sales and customer service professionals. In describing how her sense of satisfaction might apply to her personal definition of success, she identified three tangible rewards: 1) contributing to the success of others through her teaching, 2) being recognized for those contributions, and 3) enjoying a certain amount of fame.

What does success mean to you?

1. _____
2. _____
3. _____
4. _____
5. _____

For you to truly succeed, you must identify your burning passion, your vision. It's no use waiting for a level playing field. In life, you make your own level playing field. Don't be one of those people who let life pass them by. The purpose of this book is to give you the tools and a road map for your success NOW!

> *Find a purpose in life so big it will challenge every capacity to be at your best.*
> —David O. Mckay, Mormon Missionary (1873-1970)

Success Is About Participating

The one thing I know for sure about success is that to achieve it you have to be a participant. You must be prepared to take action, be a player. Success is about being willing to take the journey no matter where it might lead you. It involves being able to stay on course, to take the bumps, the knocks and the inevitable twists and turns that will come your way on your journey. Writer Lynn Gerald said, "If the sun can shine after the darkest storm, so can we."

People who watch on the sidelines of life and wait for others to make things happen for them will never achieve what they are looking for. Success will not come to you; you have to hunt it down. You have to create the conditions, and design the plays and the purpose of what it is you want to achieve and become.

Become a risk taker: Get out of your comfort zone

Only those who dare to fail greatly can ever achieve greatly.
—Robert Kennedy, statesman

Success means stretching your limits every time you are in the game. Are you prepared to go after what you want in life, to sacrifice and pay the price? These are the qualities that set apart the average individual from the world's achievers and winners. The average person frequently worries about the risks and the consequences involved in doing something different in order to achieve a better life. Successful people don't worry about the risks involved. They jump right in and *do whatever it takes*. They are comfortable with who they are and realize that despite setbacks along the way, obstacles are just part of the journey.

There can be no success without setbacks. In fact, I believe that if you haven't experienced enough setbacks, failure or rejection in your life, it usually means you have not been living life as it should be lived, taken enough risks, and ultimately have not been as successful as you could have been. This is an indication that you have lived passively on the sidelines as a spectator instead of in the center of the action—as a player!

Every successful person from Henry Ford to Oprah Winfrey to Michael Jordan to Elizabeth Taylor to Donald Trump will tell stories about risks they have taken and the failures they have experienced in order to achieve the success they have come to enjoy. Thomas Watson Sr., founder of IBM, said, "If you want to double your success rate, you must first be prepared to double your rate of failure."

I believe you have to get uncomfortable before you can become comfortable with who you truly are and with what you truly want. Let me explain that statement. What I mean is that you have to be prepared to get out of your comfort zone. For many people that involves change, and change makes some people feel uncomfortable.

I know that change is not easy. My personal experiences with change will testify to that. The one constant feature of change is that we can run from it, we can resist it, we can hide from it, but eventually it will find us. My personal philosophy is this: if we resist change we will fail. If we accept change we will survive, but for those of us who are prepared to embrace change, then I believe we will succeed.

Business consultant and author Nido Qubein said it best: "Some people find change more threatening than challenging. They see it as the destroyer of the familiar and the comfortable, rather than the creator of the new and exciting."

Believe in Your Success

It is not who you think you are, or even who you think you are not that really determines success. It's who you think you are becoming.

—Doug Firebaugh, professional speaker

Believe in the Possibilities

No matter how much you want to succeed, if you do not believe you will, then success will not happen for you. Novelist W. Somerset Maugham once said, "It's funny about life. If you refuse to accept anything but the very best, you will often get it!"

Success is not about how deserving you think you are, how lucky you have been, or how well intentioned or educated you may be. Success is about a total, absolute, unequivocal belief in yourself and your abilities. It is about having an unshakable mindset and positive attitude. If you want to change your outside world, you have to be prepared to change your inside world first. You must imagine and believe success will happen for you. There is a Chinese proverb that states, "Your first victory has to be over yourself." Whatever success means to you, if you don't believe it with all your heart, it will never happen in your mind. Without true belief, your dreams will fade, your hopes will evaporate, and you will settle for a world of mediocrity, regretting what might have been.

For over 25 years, I lived with a very severe stuttering disability. I tried many times to overcome this handicap, but always without success. There were many underlying reasons why I had not been successful, but ultimately the one reason it really came down to was that I did not believe in myself. I did not believe in my ability to overcome the challenge my speech presented. In fact, if I am totally honest with myself and with you, and it pains me to admit it, I probably used my disability to justify other failures and rejections. I was scared that if I did do something about my speech, I would not have any more excuses or a crutch to fall back on if I failed in other things. Which brings me to another point: Success is based on being honest, particularly with yourself.

In life, we can either use our obstacles as an excuse to fail, or we can use them as a catalyst or reason to succeed.

Accept Support

Finding a belief in yourself can happen in many ways. For me, it came by way of a person named Andrew Bell who made me believe it was possible to achieve anything I wanted. You see, for so many years, I wanted to do something about my speech, but was never willing to pay the price and make the necessary sacrifices. Then one night back in 1986, I was channel surfing when I stumbled across a television profile of Andrew Bell and his alternative approach to 'curing' a stutter (or stammer as it is widely called in the United Kingdom). For some reason, Mr. Bell and his philosophy resonated with me. I learned that to overcome my stuttering, I had to first believe in myself. The same is true whether you want to overcome a stutter, increase your sales or improve your relationships…

Nothing happens by itself. John Cappaz coined the expression that the only free lunch is in mousetraps! This is so true.

Don't Depend on Luck

When someone is successful, there's always a feeling that they were lucky. Luck plays a part, sure, but to be successful, you must have iron discipline. You must have energy and hunger and desire and honesty.

—Faye Dunaway, actor

We make our own luck. Some people may be lucky temporarily, but successful people don't rely on luck. Luck is a consequence of working hard and working 'smart,' of taking risks and trying new things. The law of averages states that if you try something enough times, you will eventually succeed. You may call that lucky in the process, and that is okay; nonetheless, people who go through life relying on luck alone will always be just spectators in life and success.

Sadly, I recently read that in North America, 67 percent of people surveyed stated they were relying on winning the lottery or having a big win at a casino or a sporting event to secure their future. Forgetting the moral issue regarding gambling here (and I know for some people it is a highly charged issue), the point is how sad it is that people are banking their futures on being lucky. The odds on winning are so low. Luck or chance may happen to us along the way, and that is a bonus, but if you rely on luck alone, you will be waiting a long time.

Face Your Fears

The brave person is not the person without fears, but the person who acts in spite of fear.

—Brian Tracy, author and trainer
in sales, goal setting and success

Change is possible for all of us, but the one factor we all have to let go of is our fear, and that is easier said than done, right? Did you know that fear is the one element in our lives that can stop us cold in our tracks? It can ruin ambition and dreams. It can eat away at us emotionally, physically and mentally, and can destroy our life in so many ways if we let it, but fear is ever-present in our lives. I often ask my audiences how many of them have ever been paralyzed with fear. The reaction on their faces says it all. I would argue that every one of us has experienced incredible fear at some time, in some way, so we all know what it feels like. Fear can stop us from moving forward, prevent us from stepping out of our comfort zone, and make us go to extraordinary lengths to avoid situations we don't want to face.

Identifying our fears is the first step in facing them. For some people, it is the fear of public speaking. For others, it is the fear of rejection, the fear of losing, the fear of the unknown, the fear of change, the fear of failure, and for some, even the fear of success! My greatest fear was of embarrassing myself with my severe stuttering and my inability to speak. That fear basically controlled my life for over 25 years. The fear itself took on a life of its own.

I believe we have two choices with our fears: we can choose to ignore them hoping they will go away, which for most of us will not happen, or we can try to better understand them. If we face fear instead of running away from it, a magical thing happens: we discover that fear is really a coward. When you finally come to that realization, a whole new world of possibilities and opportunities opens up. Doubt is suddenly replaced by confidence; hesitation is replaced by an urgency to do those things we used to fear. Our limitations of the past become the opportunities of the future.

Remember always that on the other side of fear lies a pot of gold called freedom. I wish I had known all those years ago that there was light at the end of the tunnel. If only I had been willing to have courage and to take that all-important first step! That first step is the hardest step you will ever have to take, but trust me—once you have taken it, each subsequent step gets easier.

Exercise: My biggest fears

List the FIVE greatest fears that are holding you back from success:

1. _____
2. _____
3. _____
4. _____
5. _____

Congratulations! By labeling your fears, you have taken the first powerful step in achieving success. Writing down your fears, having them in front of you on paper and being totally honest with yourself, may be the most important exercise you do in this whole book.

Tackle Your Fears

Most people are paralyzed with fear. Overcome it and you take charge of your life and your world.
—Mark Victor Hansen, co-author of *New York Times* #1 best-selling *Chicken Soup for the Soul* series

After doing the powerful exercise in the previous section, your next step is finding a way to press on despite your fears, and this involves confronting them. The process requires a high degree of discipline and courage. Prior to going to Scotland for what would turn out to be a life-changing speech course, I lived with the fear that when I tried to speak, my stuttering would prevent me from getting my words out and humiliate me. I believed I wouldn't be able to get my ideas across, and that people would make fun of me. However, I returned from the course with a whole new method for how to speak and techniques for controlling my stuttering. My first task was to take on my fear directly. That meant throwing myself into situations where speaking had previously been a particular challenge for me. To support my confidence, I started with my least challenging fear and built from there.

Exercise: Tackling my fears

In this next exercise, take each of the five fears you identified for yourself in the previous exercise, and one by one, consider how you will tackle them. Challenge your fears, stand up to them, and you will see from this dynamic exercise how you can rise up and overcome what is holding you back. Learn also to celebrate your success. Reward yourself for each end result and success.

> *Obstacles can't stop you. Problems can't stop you. Most of all, other people can't stop you. Only you can stop you.*
> —Jeffrey Gitomer, sales trainer and author of *The Sales Bible* and *Customer Satisfaction Is Worthless: Customer Loyalty Is Priceless*

MY ACTION PLAN
Fear #1:

_____

How I will tackle my fear:

_____
_____

Desired result:

_____
_____

Fear #2:

_____

How I will tackle my fear:

_____

_____

Desired result:

_____

_____

Fear #3:

_____

How I will tackle my fear:

_____

_____

Desired result:

_____

_____

Fear #4:

_____

How I will tackle my fear:

_____

_____

Desired result:

_____

_____

Fear #5:

_____

How I will tackle my fear:

_____

_____

Desired result:

_____

_____

Four Principles for Success

In my presentations and seminars, I am often asked, "How do you find the courage to confront your fears?" Here are **four** principles that have worked for me over the years.

Vision

Always have a clear vision of where you want to go and what you want to achieve in your life. NEVER let go of that dream. Create your vision, articulate your vision, and then execute your vision!

Courage

Grab onto the courage, inner strength and conviction to take action on those burning desires and thoughts you have inside you. Have the courage of your convictions always and do what is right for you. Sir Winston Churchill, a man of destiny and history who knew a thing or two about courage, used to say, "Courage is rightly considered the foremost of all virtues because upon it, all others depend."

Responsibility

Take full and total responsibility for your actions in life. Do not wait for other people to come along and make the 'good stuff' happen for you. Take control of your life and make the good stuff happen yourself. You alone must risk that first step. Look at yourself in the mirror; be true to the person you see there.

Commitment

Show 100 percent commitment in everything you do. Be the master of your own ship! You can have great intentions, desire and even determination to face your challenges and to succeed, but without full and true commitment, your dreams will fade away and die, and you will always struggle to turn the noblest of intentions into actions and results. Pat Riley, the famous basketball coach from the NBA, once said, "There are only two options regarding commitment: you're either in or you're out. There's no such thing as in-between."

Attitude Is Everything

Ability is what you are capable of doing. Motivation determines what you do. Attitude determines how well you do it.
—Lou Holtz, American college football coach

Many good books have been written about attitude. I am going to spend a little more time on this subject as it is near and dear to my heart and because it is one of the single most important attributes of successful people—if not the most important one. Without a positive outlook, without having optimism about your future, without a 'can do' attitude, you will not achieve whatever success means to you.

Attitude is one of the few things that we control in our lives. We know we cannot always control circumstances, situations or conditions that arise, but we can control how we react to them. Attitude is where you get your strength to survive and prevail, especially in times of crisis and adversity. Attitude separates the people who have the will and confidence to succeed, from the people who will either continually fail or merely achieve mediocrity. Look around at people you admire and respect. I would bet that most of them, if not all of them, share one common trait: a positive attitude toward life and the pursuit of success. Stuff happens to all of us, some good and some not so good, but the winners in life are those who stay positive, even through those inevitable tough times.

Seeing Mr. Bell on TV in 1986 was the cue to me that one of the key things holding me back in my pursuit of success over my stutter was my attitude. That moment was my call to action. And in his course, he taught us to believe in ourselves no matter what. Andrew Bell used to say, "Have a 'can do' attitude! Show people the confident and successful person you are." Much of the time, our thoughts direct what we ultimately become, and what we achieve.

Thoughts become words, words become actions, actions become habit, habit becomes character, and character becomes destiny.
                                                            —Frank Outlaw

---

A few years ago, a friend of mine, Karen, was diagnosed with cancer. Early diagnosis and treatment enabled her to successfully put the cancer into remission. She attributed her success to God and the love, help and support of family, friends and, of course, her doctors, but the overriding factor of significance, according to her doctors, was her faith and positive mindset that she would beat her illness. How many times have you heard, read of, or maybe even experienced first-hand the power of a positive attitude?

Attitude also dictates what we show of ourselves to the world and how we will be perceived. Before the speech course, my attitude was very negative and my self-worth and self-esteem were low, and that's what I showed to the world. People did not want to be around me, and looking back at it now, who could blame them? I, too, would have run a mile to get away from me back then! I am sure we have all met people who carry an attitude that the world is against them; they perceive that life is so hard on them. But think of people you know who are happy and optimistic, who see the good in every situation, who see opportunity in every obstacle; they are the people we want to be around.

Attitude plays a crucial role in everything we do. It not only determines our actions and directs the way that we think about ourselves, it also sends out a strong message about us. It can make the difference between winning and losing, success and failure. We can choose to be negative toward life and challenges, or we can choose to be positive. A positive attitude is infectious. It lights a fire inside you and in others around you. Nothing can stop a person with a positive attitude, and nothing in life will stop a person more quickly than having a negative one—let's be crystal clear on that. Think about it. When you meet people who have a positive attitude, what is your impression of them? They are confident and know what they are doing. You probably would like to get to know them better, or wish you could be more like them.

I have found, over the years, that to change our attitude we must first change our thought process and beliefs. We must stop listening to people with negative thoughts, the people who can bring us down.

A great attitude is your secret weapon in your pursuit of success. It gives you the staying power to persist, the confidence to try new things, the courage to believe in yourself when the going gets tough, and the mindset to believe that you can achieve anything you want in life and grow to your full potential. The difference between a truly successful person and an average or unsuccessful one lies in their attitude. Successful people have the mentality that they can do anything and that nothing is beyond their reach. That outlook is embedded in their whole being. Since they are positive, they send several messages: they are comfortable with themselves; they know where they are going; they are people to do business with; and they will deliver. Their comfort level puts others at ease.

It's your attitude: Choose one that's positive

You can't put a price on a truly positive attitude, and the good news is that you can change your attitude at any time! You have full and complete control over your attitude and it can be worked on because it's not set in stone. You have the power to change how you feel and act RIGHT NOW. Unless you let them, nobody can control that except you. It takes work and daily actions, but it is your choice how others perceive you.

Mark worked for a national company selling insurance and financial services, but he was not doing well. His sales were down and his company was dissatisfied with his performance, as was Mark. Moreover, the bottom line in sales is that your numbers must be there. Other factors do certainly come into the equation, but at the end of the day you will be judged on your numbers, and the numbers do not lie.

When I met Mark at one of my presentations, he was in danger of losing his job. He explained his situation to me and asked me how he could get out of his slump and save his job. After getting to know him a little better, I recognized some areas that I felt were holding him back. Mostly, Mark had lost his focus. Instead of staying on target with his own results, he had become preoccupied with what other people were doing in the company. As a result, he had become envious and somewhat resentful of the success-ful performers. When I asked him what he envied about these people, he said they seemed confident and self-assured, that they had an aura about them. So confident they were about themselves, it seemed that nothing fazed them. Basically, they had great attitudes.

Over the next few weeks and months, I had Mark identify the areas in which he needed to improve through a self-analysis process, similar to the exercise in 'attitude opportunities' that follows. He found such trouble spots as: negativity toward others, low self-esteem, poor body language, and a preference for making a sale rather than adding value and being of service to his clients.

I had him focus all his energies on a positive outlook and recognizing him-self as a valuable asset to the organization and to his clients. Mark worked really hard. He did what was asked of him and more. Slowly, he started to turn his life and career around, just by taking small steps and setting a dif-ferent goal each day.

Changing your attitude is like changing a habit. It takes time and effort. For Mark, who was dedicated to changing, each and every day became a great day. He now funneled all his energies into positive thinking. There was no more worrying about what everybody else was doing, no more idle gossip about people around him, no more being envious and jealous. As Mark's attitude began to change, his demeanor altered, and do you know what happened? People in his office and in his personal life started to take notice of him. As he became more confident, he became more popular, and people wanted to 'hang out' with him. New clients wanted to deal with him because of his positive attitude. Because he became re-energized and refocused, his sales improved dramatically.

> *Our business in life is not to get ahead of others, but to get ahead of ourselves—to break our own records, to outstrip our yesterday by our today.*
>
> —Stewart B. Johnson

There was nothing magical or mysterious in what Mark did. He just made a few minor adjustments in the way he perceived others. Having the correct mindset and attitude made all the difference.

Exercise: Attitude opportunities

Think about a time when you were 'on,' when you knew you were unstoppable. What was your attitude like? How were you showing yourself to the people around you?

What about a time when you were struggling and feeling negative? How was your attitude showing itself? How was that impacting the situation?

In what areas in your life do you feel a better attitude could impact your success?

What steps can you take to improve your overall attitude? Ask yourself the following questions:

- Do you wake up in the morning feeling great and excited about the day ahead? Or is it an inconvenience to get out of bed sometimes and to have to face the day?

- Do you see the good in people and in life in general, or do you see the bad? Is the glass half-full or half-empty?

- Do you consider yourself fortunate to be alive? Are you genuinely happy for other people's success and achievements? Or do you spend your time whining about your situation ("Woe is me") and being jealous?

- Do you see your life as one of opportunity, where you add value to people's lives? Or do you feel you are faced with insurmountable challenges? Or are you simply out for what you can get?

- Do you always seek the solution in everything? Or do you only see the problem?

- Do you have an air of confidence about yourself where nothing much ever fazes you? Do you look like one of those people who know where they are going? Do you make other people feel good about themselves? Are people drawn to you when you walk into a room? Do people want to be your friend and do business with you? Or do you feel down all the time, feel life is treating you badly, feel nothing good ever happens to you? Do people avoid you, or not want to do business with you? Do you try to bring people down instead of picking them up?

These are pretty tough questions to confront yourself with, and for some people there could be some real truths revealed. These questions could be a wake-up call. Be honest with yourself. Complete the exercise with courage.

Your attitude drives the goal

The good news, as I mentioned earlier, is that your attitude can be changed at any time; however, you must not switch your good attitude on and off when it suits you. You can, but people will see through it. People will see that you are putting it on and that it is not genuine. A positive attitude must become part of you. It must be with you 24/7. Your positive attitude must become your new habit. Yes, you can have a bad day, but your attitude will define how quickly you bounce back.

I always wear a lapel pin that reads 'Attitude' as a constant reminder for myself. It is my little badge of courage that tells me that as long as I keep my attitude positive, things are going to be okay. You would not believe the reaction I get. Perfect strangers come up to me at airports, on the street, at my programs, from everywhere, to ask me about the lapel pin. They make a comment about attitude or become animated and excited about sharing their own story with me. To this day, the reaction this little pin gets still amazes me. (Visit my website at www.cmarcus.com to order one of these pins for yourself.)

Jane, a colleague of mine, told me a great story, that relates to attitude and having a positive outlook on life. Jane is an active marathon runner, participating in about 15 races a year all over the world. (Just thinking of that many races makes me feel exhausted!) Jane enjoys her running, traveling to new places and meeting new people. She tells me that before a race she gets 'psyched.' After months of training and preparation, her adrenaline peaks. At most of her marathons, the crowd is large for the first mile or so, and everybody is cheering like crazy, wishing all the competitors well. Their energy keeps her pumped. Then the crowd starts to thin out. In some places there is hardly anybody there at all to cheer on the runners. It gets lonely in that stretch. Then, in the last mile or so, the crowds grow again and everybody seems to be coaxing her forward. Their encouragement reinforces her confidence to succeed.

Jane motivates herself by not thinking of the enormity of the 26 miles that she has to run to complete her race. She mentally focuses on one step at a time. Every step takes her closer to her destination, and by centering on one step, the task at hand seems less daunting for her. Those steps then quickly turn into miles, and the distance does not seem psychologically so far to her.

Isn't life like running a marathon race in a lot of ways? In the beginning, we have people cheering us on and encouraging us to succeed, and near the finish line, people are there again cheering us forward. But in between, during that long haul, it can be lonely and it can take true grit to keep going. The things that keep us going are our attitude, our focus and vision of the finish line, and taking it one step at a time.

Think about the powerful and chilling words of Viktor E. Frankl in *Man's Search for Meaning* to know that attitude plays a role even in the most horrific of events in history:

We who lived in concentration camps can remember the men who walked through the huts comforting others, giving away their last piece of bread. They may have been few in number, but they offer sufficient proof that everything can be taken from a man but one thing: the last of the human freedoms—to choose one's attitude in any given set of circumstances, to choose one's own way.

Ideas for developing a positive attitude and making every day a great day

- Wake up every morning grateful, hopeful and optimistic about the day. The old saying holds true: Today is the first day of the rest of your life.

- Do not be envious, jealous or resentful. It is unproductive and a waste of your time. Instead, be happy for people who are doing well. Go out of your way to help those who are not as positive and successful as you are.

- Think forward. Don't think about what 'might have been' in the past because it will complicate matters and get in the way of what you can achieve in the future. We should all think about our past, learn from it, and then move on. People with a great positive attitude know this well. As Satchel Page, American baseball great, said, "It's nice to look back, but don't stare." People with great attitudes are forward thinkers.

- Spend your time with positive people. I've mentioned this before, but it is so important. Who you associate with, and spend your time with, will help determine a greater part of your attitude. Don't waste your time with people who are negative. Choose positive people who inspire you and from whom you can learn. Stay away from the dream stealers at all costs.

- Eliminate as much stress and worry in your life as possible. Pursue a pleasant hobby that relaxes you, and watch your health and diet. I walk a lot and jog. It gives me time to think. I enjoy the fresh air even in the winter months, and here in Canada we have intense winter months! I get a lot of my positive ideas and energy from my walks. Learn to develop a healthy mind, perspective and attitude about yourself and about life.

- Learn to lighten up and not to take yourself or life so seriously. I don't mean that you should not be focused and committed to your goals, but sometimes you just have to 'go with the flow.' Be grateful for everything you have. Be comfortable and proud of who you are and where you are going.

- Make time to identify five people whom you admire. Choose people who are enthusiastic and passionate. Find a way to contact them, call, write, ask them out to lunch, or ask them to be your mentor. Find out what makes them tick and how they remain so positive even when the going gets tough.

Take time to reconnect with people you have been negative with in the past. Think about people to whom you have said things that you may have regretted. Make contact with them and show them your new positive attitude. It takes courage and being a BIG person to ask people to give you a second chance—most people will, not everybody, but most. Make that second chance count.

- Challenge yourself in everything you say and do. By challenging yourself, you discover things about yourself that you never even knew you were capable of doing. By challenging yourself, you develop confidence, and confidence leads to self-worth, self-discovery, self-esteem, and to a positive attitude.

Some people will argue that even if they have a great attitude, it does not necessarily mean that they will be successful. This is true. Nobody can guarantee 100 percent success. What I will steadfastly guarantee, though, is that if you 'think you can,' and you have an unshakable attitude, a positive outlook on life, along with a clear definition of success, you will certainly accomplish more than you would otherwise. You will have a greater chance of complete success; in most cases, you will be unstoppable. A great attitude does not happen by itself. Henry Ford said, "You can't build a reputation on what you are going to do." A positive attitude comes from belief and taking action, as well as your dedication to working on it. Note those two words: BELIEF and ACTION.

Attitude
by Charles Swindell

The longer I live
The more I realize the impact of attitude on life.
Attitude, to me, is more important than the past,
Than education,
Than money,
Than circumstances,
Than failures,
Than success,
Than what other people think or say or do.
It is more important than appearance,
Giftedness or skill.
It will make or break an organization,
A school, a home.
The remarkable thing is we have a choice every day
Regarding the attitude we will embrace for that day.
We cannot change our past.
We cannot change the fact that people will act in a certain way.
We cannot change the inevitable.
The only thing we can do
Is play the string we have.
And that is our attitude.
I am convinced that life is 10 percent what happens to me
And 90 percent how I react to it.
And so it is with you

Set Goals

We all know about setting goals. Most of the time we set them with great intentions. We have high hopes for success, and we get excited. We join that health club to get in shape or to lose those few extra pounds. We make that career change, doing that one special thing we have always dreamed about. We all want to achieve our dreams, hopes and aspirations, but for one reason or another we frequently never see our important goals through to action. Goals, as we all know, are commonly set at New Year's, and soon afterwards, are forgotten.

Highly successful people have the ability, vision and firmness of purpose to set and review their goals regularly. It is one of the things that separate them from the pack. They know that *success is not a spectator sport*, and they know that vision without action is just a daydream, but vision and action combined is a recipe for success.

Philosopher and author Jim Rohn said this about goals: *If you go to work on your goals, your goals will go to work on you; if you go to work on your plan, your plan will go to work on you. Whatever good things we build end up building us.*

Remember that the smallest of actions is always better than the noblest of intentions.

How about setting some goals for yourself right now! The following is a formula I have found particularly effective for setting and achieving my own goals.

A 10–part formula for setting and achieving your goals

1. Sit down NOW and spend some quality time by yourself in a quiet room making out your goal list. Do not take this first step lightly. This is your blueprint, your road map to success. Give it the time and respect it deserves. Ask yourself what it is you really want to achieve and what is really important to you. Are your expectations realistic? Are you prepared to sacrifice and pay the necessary price to achieve these goals? These are tough questions, but you MUST take the time and be really honest with yourself. I'm sometimes amazed that many people spend more time watching television or planning their next family vacation than they do planning their own future! Be very serious about your goals because they will not just happen by themselves. You CAN and must make them happen yourself.

2. Write your goals down on paper and put them somewhere you can see them at least once a day. There is nothing more powerful than having your goals in black and white and in front of you. Brian Tracy said, "Goals in writing are dreams with deadlines." Be imaginative, and make the list as long as you want. There are no limitations.

3. Break your goals down into the categories and time frames suited to your needs and objectives. Most of your goals will be individual, but also set some with your spouse or significant other. Some examples: financial goals, career goals, spiritual goals, health goals, family goals and personal development goals. Make your own list and define what is important to you and your future!

4. Prioritize. You can have as many goals as you like, but think realistically—don't let your goals overwhelm you. Pick out the three or four most important and essential ones and set those with a tighter timeline.

5. Do not worry if you have to change your plan and re-evaluate your goals from time to time. You can start or retool your goals at *any* time, not just at the beginning of the year. There are no set rules; you make your own. Reassess your goals daily, weekly or monthly. There is no right or wrong way to set your goals. We all have different time frames and agendas, so do what is right for you. The most important thing is to never lose your FOCUS. Nothing is set in stone, but remember, it is also not set in sand. Be flexible, but not wishy-washy.

6. Make yourself a sign or something visible to you that will keep you focused. There are times when things are not going to go your way, or when you may feel like giving up. I have a big sign in my office where my goals are posted that displays two simple but profound words: PERSISTENCE and COMMITMENT. These words keep me focused and on track. What will motivate you to keep going, to persevere when you feel like giving up, or when you are having a bad day?

7. Join the 3 percent club. That's right, generally only 3 percent of people in the world will see their goals through to achievement. As amazing as that sounds, it is true. That has been proven in survey after survey, worldwide. Would you like to join that elite group? What is there to stop you? The only person who can stop you is you.

8. Look long, act short. My philosophy about meeting goals is to have a long-term focus, but short-term objectives. It is the little steps that keep us going, those little victories that stop us from becoming frustrated by the short-term setbacks that will occur from time to time. Do not be afraid of taking a few steps backwards sometimes. That is okay as long as you are also taking more steps forward, ultimately heading in the right direction. You will get to where you want to be in the end. Trust me. You can never be a winner in life unless you have the courage to face obstacles along the way.

9. Share your goals with people you trust and whose opinion you value: family, friends, loved ones, work colleagues. I have always found this to be an effective way of staying focused, accountable and positive. Of

course you will share different goals with different people, and you may choose to keep some very personal goals to yourself, but in general, I truly believe that sharing your goals works. Try it, and see if it works for you.

10. Finally, have fun with your goals. Achieving them should be a treat, not a chore, but also realize they will not happen by themselves. You must be fully committed to achieving what it is you want in life. It is great to believe and to be inspired and motivated, but it will not happen for you unless you ACT upon your goals and take a positive step every single day.

Treat your goals with respect and give them your full attention, time and energy. They will bring you the rewards and success you desire.

Give Yourself a Target

Canadian-born actor Jim Carrey is today one of the highest paid and most famous celebrities in the world, but success did not come easily. He had to leave school in grade nine to help his parents make ends meet when his father lost his job. One of his first jobs was as a janitor.

Carrey struggled for many years to find his way, but he never lost his sense of humor or his determination to succeed, even when things got really tough for him. He was told many times he would never make it in show business, but he had set his heart on success. He eventually left his home near Toronto and moved to Los Angeles to 'make it' and to perfect his craft. During the next years of frequent rejection and loneliness, Carrey always believed in himself. To keep himself motivated and focused, he wrote himself a check for $10 million and posted it where he could see it every day; that is what he wanted to earn per movie when he became a big star. This was a bold vision for anybody, let alone an unknown comedian struggling to make ends meet. It became almost an obsession with him. Today, Jim Carrey earns well over $20 million per movie in Hollywood, exceeding even his own expectations!

Beyond his stardom, what makes Jim Carrey special and real to so many people is that he shows us his human side. He shares his failures as well as his successes. People feel they can relate to him because he shows the public his vulnerable side. He earns our respect because he is not afraid to try something new, to take a chance. Yes, he is zany and offbeat sometimes, but you have to admire his nerve. And, to so many of us, besides his fame, he just seems like a regular guy. The only difference with Jim Carrey is that there are not too many *regular* guys who earn $20 million for a few weeks of work.

What are your goals?

What goal or vision do you have for yourself? It doesn't have to have a $10 million price tag on it. It can be anything you want, big or small. Write down something symbolic or especially meaningful about that goal. Put it somewhere so you can see it every day. Focus on it, but don't lose sight of your true self in the journey.

Exercise: The 12 things I want to achieve in the next 12 months

Take a few minutes now to think about the big things you want to accomplish over the next 12 months. While there is no magic number to how many goals you should have, you are better to go with a small number of high-impact goals that you can focus on and achieve. Having too many goals may overwhelm you and result in nothing getting done. The key is to be flexible. Remember: nothing is set in stone.

1. _____
2. _____
3. _____
4. _____
5. _____
6. _____
7. _____
8. _____
9. _____
10. _____

11. _____
12. _____

Now doesn't it feel better to have your goals down on paper? Most people do not even get to this stage with their goals, so you are already ahead of the pack.

Goals Are About a Plan of Action

Don't agonize—organize!!
—Florence R. Kennedy

Anything worth doing is worth doing well and deserves a well-thought-out plan of action. This involves setting goals, and not just one goal, but a number of shorter term, interim goals.

Breaking down a seemingly impossible task into smaller steps will make it seem less overwhelming and more achievable. For example, if you want to lose some weight, the idea of dieting to lose 50 pounds may seem too much for you to envisage. Why not break it down to losing just a pound at a time, then set a goal of, let's say, one or two pounds a week. (Be sure to consult your doctor for expert advice on the appropriate target.) Combining these goals with a positive attitude will put you on the road to success.

Exercise: Setting your action plan

Take a few minutes now to take one of the goals you identified in the previous exercise and break it down into those manageable chunks.

What is my overall goal?_____

Date goal started (enter today's date!): _____

Target date for completion: _____

set goals

Interim goals/action plan:

1. _____ Target Date: _____
2. _____ Target Date: _____
3. _____ Target Date: _____
4. _____ Target Date: _____
5. _____ Target Date: _____

The Vijay Singh story

Vijay Singh is a world-class professional golfer from the beautiful island of Fiji in the South Pacific. He is not as well known perhaps as Tiger Woods, but he has the respect and admiration of his fellow professionals for his dignity and his gentlemanly sportsmanship.

Vijay Singh grew up on an island where golf was not a common sport; in fact, the international golf events were not even shown live on television. Singh used to watch taped highlights of the annual US Masters event, one of the most prestigious golf events in the world, while he dreamed of one day walking up to the 18th green in Augusta, Georgia, on the final day of play, to the applause of the crowd. People thought he was crazy, but he had a dream.

In 1986, he moved to the United States to pursue his dream. He worked his way up the golfing ranks and became a professional golfer, winning tournaments and carving out a good living for himself and his family, but never winning the big one—the Masters. He somehow always fell short of his goal.

By 1999, Singh's dream had become an obsession with him. That year, he hired a conditioning coach and changed his diet. He watched taped highlights of every tournament he played that year and every Masters he had previously played. He analyzed every shot and every putt he made. Then he visualized himself on every hole at the 2000 Masters and imagined himself on that 18th hole, winning the Masters in style and putting on the famous green jacket that is presented to all the winners. For all of 1999 he basically focused on nothing else.

At the 2000 US Masters, Singh made a good start in the tournament. The first two days of play had gone well. As he left the clubhouse on the third and final day of play, his nine-year-old son taped a note on his father's clubs that said, "Papa, trust your swing."

Singh listened to the wisdom of a nine-year-old. With his family at his side and his nation back home now watching the event live and urging him on, he went on to be the 2000 US Masters champion. Almost 20 years of effort paid off.

When asked later what had made the difference in 2000, he simply said, "I wanted it badly this year and was prepared to make the necessary sacrifices. I was prepared to pay the price, so how can you not go out there and win when your son has such faith in you!"

How many of us have a dream or a goal that we—and maybe many others—feel may be unachievable? My question to you is, are you willing to pay the price that Vijay Singh did to achieve his goal, to live out his dream? Do you have people in your life who believe in you, or who trust your swing?

Demonstrate Flexibility

Goals are meant to be flexible. This is where most people fail. They set wonderful goals for themselves, but show no flexibility if results do not occur right away. They become discouraged, and their hopes and dreams just fade away. Do not be one of those people. If your goal is not on track, you may need to adjust the target or perhaps retool your goal.

Do a regular progress check

It is important to check how you are doing along the way in order to make the necessary course corrections before it's too late. Remember: look long, but act short! Have a 7, 14, 21, 30, 60, 90, 120 and 365-day plan for taking stock of how you are doing.

Reward yourself for your accomplishments, no matter how small they seem. Do not beat yourself up if things go wrong. This is an opportunity to take stock, learn from the experience and adjust as necessary. What will you do if you miss your target? How will you adjust?

Don't Procrastinate

If you procrastinate when faced with a big difficult problem, break the problem into parts, and handle one part at a time.
—Robert Collier, author of *Riches Within Your Reach*

One of the biggest problems I find people have these days is that they procrastinate. They put off doing those tasks and things they need to do today until tomorrow, which then turns into the day after...and the day after that. Does that pattern sound familiar? I think if most people were honest with themselves, they would admit that they procrastinate from time to time. It is only human nature. As I share a story in my presentations about when I used to put off doing things, I often ask the question, "How many fellow procrastinators do we have in the audience today?" I usually see some brave and honest people put up their hands, even if a little reluctantly. Then I say, "We are among friends here today. Be honest with yourself. How many of you really procrastinate?" A sea of hands go up with a little laughter and even a sigh of relief, as though the big secret was finally out.

For many years I was a master procrastinator. I was always dreaming of yesterday, worrying about tomorrow, and trying to get through the day by going through the motions, rather than assuming the more worthy challenge of accomplishing what had to be done.

Successful people do not procrastinate. They are decisive, they value time, and they squeeze every ounce of joy and energy they can from the day at hand. They make each and every day productive. William Arthur Ward said, "Our past gives us memories and experiences, our present gives us opportunities and challenges, and our future gives us vision and hope." Time is our greatest commodity. Each of us has the same 86,400 seconds in a 24-hour day. How we choose to use that time will determine how successful we will be.

How do you know if you procrastinate? Here are some telltale signs. Check the ones that apply to you.

[　]　You put off making decisions.

[　]　You make excuses for not finishing that project on time.

[　]　You are not very disciplined at organizing around your home and/or office.

[　]　You have a pile of papers in your office not filed, just building up.

[　]　You cannot seem to throw anything in the trash can, even when it is of no use to you or has been stashed away in a file, unused, for over six months.

[　]　You have big boxes around the house to store the stuff you have not filed. (Then you know you have a big problem!)

Clear Out the Clutter

'Effective time management' is one of the hottest professional development topics today. Workshops and presentations on the subject are sought out and offered to employees by corporations of all sizes. Individuals fill classes on this subject at their local community college or learning center. Some of my speaking colleagues only speak on this one subject. It should come as no surprise that effective time management is one of the keys to success. And one of the important factors in time management is cleaning up the messes in your life by eliminating the clutter and junk that builds up in your office, your home and your car.

I believe that having order in your life eliminates stress and makes you better able to focus on your goals. Think about the panic you feel and time you waste when you can't find something. I am not saying that you have to be obsessive or a neat freak to have that order in your life. Just take a few extra moments to file away things instead of letting them become a pile in the corner of your office.

In building my speaking and training business, I quickly realized I needed a system to cope with everything or it would overwhelm me. I could not bring myself to throw anything away. I would file something just for the sake of filing it, and didn't have a logical system. When I went to retrieve something, I inevitably could not find it, which would frustrate me. I knew I had a problem and sought advice from people who were experts at this sort of thing. They told me to evaluate every piece of information I receive in the mail or via e-mail or fax and ask myself, "Do I really need it or can I live without it?" They also recommended that if I filed something away, I should check every few months to evaluate whether I still needed it. I know it is hard to let go of something, but you will feel so much better if you just discipline yourself to throw things away instead of keeping them for no purpose.

Have you ever noticed how we sometimes invent so many reasons why we can't do or finish something? Really, if the truth were told, we often need only *one* reason in order to act.

Tips for avoiding procrastination

- Take 30 minutes every night, by yourself, in peace and quiet to plan your tomorrow. No interruptions or excuses. Make a TO DO list of what you want to achieve the next day. Prioritize your thoughts.

- Spend a few minutes cleaning up your work environment. Don't leave things lying around. Find a place for everything. If you can't find a place, maybe it is something that doesn't need a place at all!

- Don't put off anything you can possibly do today until tomorrow, no matter what. Make a commitment to yourself on that.

- If you're working from an office or desk, keep it clear, neat and tidy. Discipline yourself to throw away anything you don't truly need. I know this can be hard sometimes. But let it go, life will go on. File the rest neatly and quickly in the appropriate places.

- Reduce large projects into smaller manageable tasks. If you want to mow your lawn, for example, and you have a big property, break it down: do the back in the morning, take a well-deserved rest, then do the front in the afternoon.

- Don't take on more than you can handle in the time allotted, but what you commit to, finish. Think about how good you are going to feel when the task is completed. You will feel an incredible sense of accomplishment, so reward yourself.

- Always assign deadlines to whatever you commit to. I believe this is the single most important factor in accomplishing a task.

- Learn to say NO. You cannot do everything or be all things to all people. Do not take on more than you can handle. Oprah Winfrey said that one of the greatest successes in her life was having the ability to say no to people and not feeling guilty about it.

- For business, invest in a good contact or time management software system. I use *ACT*, but there is a wide variety of effective software out there. *Maximize, Goldmine* and *Paper Tiger* are others that come to mind. They are simple to manage and operate, even for people like me who are not technically adept. I could not run my business without such a system. It keeps all the information I need at my fingertips. I can even program it to remind me to follow up with clients on a regular basis, which I transfer through my computer directly to my electronic planner.

- Finally, if all else fails, hire an expert to come and coach you in your home or office, to create a plan for you, design a proper filing system, or clean up all your clutter and help you refocus. It is a worthwhile investment. Or, you can take a course or read a book on this subject; there are many available. Alternately, you can just read through this list again. Choose whichever path works for you, and good luck!

Exercise: To do list—my priorities for tomorrow

Date: _____

Task	Priority			Due Date
	A	B	C	
1.				
2.				
3.				
4.				
5.				

Remember: time is your most valuable asset. It is like the spoken word—something we can never get back. Use your time wisely. Successful people, who play the game to win, know this only too well. Well-known author John Maxwell said, "Life is like riding a taxi; whether you are going any-where or nowhere, the clock is always ticking."

Delegate

One lesson I have learned over the years about time management is to hire people who are either better qualified than I am, or to whom I can delegate or subcontract work. For example, I do not like to clean my garage. It is time-consuming for me, and like everybody else, my time is valuable. Does it not make sense for me to pay a college student or some-body who needs the extra money to do that for me? Absolutely! I win two ways: 1) It allows me to get out of something I do not like to do, and 2) it frees me up to do more important activities. I can choose to spend quality time with my family or to focus on business-related matters that have the potential to earn me a lot more money than I am paying to have my garage cleaned.

Think of some areas in your life where you could delegate some of the tasks you do not particularly like to do. You help somebody by creating employment for them—and it frees you up. You win both ways. Try it and see!

Exercise: Areas where I could delegate in order to create more time for me!

1. _____
2. _____
3. _____
4. _____
5. _____

Surround Yourself With Positive People

Avoid negative people at all costs. They are the greatest destroyers of self-confidence and self-esteem.

—Brian Tracy

We all know someone who lives life with the glass half-empty. We talked a little about people like that earlier in this book. Truly successful individuals surround themselves with people who have positive attitudes toward life and its possibilities. These people may not see things from the same perspective as you do, but they challenge you in a constructive and encouraging way.

Stay Away From the Dream Stealers

People try to rain on your parade because they have no parade of their own.

—Jeffrey Gitomer

Over the years I have learned that those who succeed in sales, the corporate boardroom, as entrepreneurs or at a personal dream or vision, stay away from negative people. Negative people destroy dreams and bring you down. They are your dream stealers. They are the people who tell you that you will not succeed and can support their predictions with many reasons. Sadly, they are often the people we have known for years and have allowed to influence us for many of those years.

When I finally made a commitment to do something about my stuttering, there were classmates in one of my self-help classes who, for whatever reason, tried to discourage me and take away my dreams by telling me I was wasting my time and money and that it would never work. I chose not to listen to them.

When I went into the field of sales, I could always spot the dream stealers in our company. They were the ones who complained and blamed their lack of success on everything except their lack of skill, strategy or focus. Always it seemed they did not have the best territory, or the boss was either against them or had another favorite. They could not celebrate the success of anyone else or encourage anyone else. When I was promoted from a sales consultant to Ontario District Manager for Nexxus Hair Products, I experienced this first-hand. The truth of the matter was that all the sales consultants had basically similar territories. The problem was not the size of the territory or the demographics, but the people who were working in those territories. Instead of wanting to improve their skills, they persisted in being negative and trying to bring everybody else down to their level. They especially tried to influence the new sales reps and steal their enthusiasm.

While you cannot avoid these negative and toxic people all the time, you have to tune them out and minimize their influence on your life. Spend the majority of your time with people who share your dreams and vision, who are supportive of you, and who have energy that is contagious.

Build a Supportive Team

It isn't the people you fire who make your life miserable, it's the people you don't.

> —Harvey Mackay, author of *Pushing the Envelope: All the Way to the Top*

"You can do it, but you can't do it alone." This is a phrase I have heard so many times, but I did not always believe it was true. I do believe it now with all my heart and soul. While we all have greatness inside of us and we all have incredible things we can achieve, in my opinion and from my experience, we cannot do it alone. We all need support, help and comfort along the way. Someone once told me, "We all need someone in our life who believes in us more than we believe in ourselves."

Think of the people in your life who have supported you and helped you get to where you are today. My guess is that you have a good solid list. Could you have done it alone, without their support and backing and love? Maybe, but would it have been as fulfilling and positive an experience? For most of us, I think the answer would be no.

Buy into the team concept! Who will be on your team?

Exercise: Pick your team

Who is on your team? What roles do they play? Coach? Cheerleader? Defensive tackle? Think about the gifts they bring to the team.

Team members   *(see exercise below)* √

_____ [   ]
_____ [   ]
_____ [   ]
_____ [   ]
_____ [   ]
_____ [   ]

What role do they play on your team?

_____
_____
_____
_____
_____

Seek Challenge

"Seek challenge" is advice I have followed often, and I have heard from many people throughout the years who have honored me by sharing their views about it. Jim Rohn said, "Don't join an easy crowd; you won't grow; go where the expectations and the demands are high." This is advice I guarantee you can take to the bank!

Exercise: Add challenge to your team

Go back to your team list above and put a checkmark (√) beside the individuals who will set high expectations and challenge you positively. If you do not have any motivating or challenging people on your list, you may want to enlist a few.

Treat Every Setback as a Valuable Learning Experience

Failure is just another opportunity to begin again more intelligently.

—Henry Ford, The Ford Motor Company

Be a Student of Success

Those who tell you they have not experienced any setbacks or failures are probably either not telling you the whole truth or they have lived incredibly unchallenging, unproductive or boring lives. You may often have heard the expression, "It is not how many times you fall down, it is how many times you pick yourself up that counts." This may be a well-used cliché, but nonetheless, it is so true. If you sat down and spoke to a number of the most successful people in business and life, you would probably find that many of them would tell stories about how they had failed over and over again before they were successful.

Be prepared to fail, sometimes over and over and over again, in your pursuit of your dreams, hopes and ambitions. One of basketball superstar Michael Jordan's most sought-after posters reads, "I've missed more than

9,000 shots in my career. I've lost almost 300 games. 26 times I've been trusted to take the game-winning shot and missed. I've failed over and over and over again in my life. And that is why I succeed."

As I look back on my personal experiences and what I have learned about the people I admire, I believe that success is roughly 80 percent failure, and the key to being successful is to not focus on the 80% failure rate but stay focused on the 20 percent success rate. You have to have the right mindset to be able to deal with rejection and not take it personally.

When I first went into sales, working for Jobar Ltd., distributors for Nexxus Hair Products, which is one of the world's leading manufacturers of professional hair-care products, I was new to the sales game. In fact, this was the first job I took on after learning to control my stutter. To learn the craft, I watched the people who were successful; I learned what made them tick, what separated them from everyone else. The answer was very simple: nothing fazed them. They were focused on what they wanted to achieve. They did not take rejection personally. They also did not accept or hear the word "No." In fact, they told me that hearing "No" represented to them a request for further information. Statistics show that it takes roughly six to eight calls or visits before a sales person makes the sale. In between, there are going to be a lot of rejections. It is not rocket science to understand that what separates mediocrity and the average sales person from the successful sales professional is the ability and attitude to hang in there, and to persevere, no matter what.

When my baby daughter Rachel had just learned how to crawl, we discovered that she loved to eat the soil in our houseplants. Go figure. Every time my wife Mary or I saw her going toward the plants, we would say to her "No, sweetheart, don't do that," and move her away from them. She would look at us with her big eyes and adorable smile and then go right back to the dirt to snack. The point is, what does "No" mean to a child? It means absolutely nothing, and is just a challenge for them to try harder. And what should "No" mean to adults when it comes to something that they really want to achieve? In each case, it means exactly the same thing—it's a challenge to try harder. We could certainly learn a lot from our children.

Learn From Those Who Failed

A pessimist sees the difficulty in every opportunity. An optimist sees the opportunity in every difficulty.
—Sir Winston Churchill

Don't worry if you've made a bad decision; we all do along the way. I have drawn so much inspiration in my life by reading about and studying people who have turned failure after failure into success, adversity into opportunity, a negative into a positive, or a seemingly hopeless situation into one of hope.

I would like to share a few examples of people who have met adversity and have gone on to tremendous success. I hope you take inspiration from them just as I have done over the years:

When he started his career, legendary dancer Fred Astaire was told by several studios in Hollywood that he was short on talent and would never make it as a dancer. He framed those rejection letters and they spurred him on. Fred Astaire is acclaimed in film history as one of the greatest dancers of his generation, performing solo and with his famous dance partner, Ginger Rogers.

Walt Disney went bankrupt five times before he created Disneyland and ultimately the Disney Corporation.

In 1962, Decca Records rejected four lads from Liverpool: John, Paul, George and Ringo. They were told, "We don't like guitar music, and it is on the way out." HMV, Columbia and Philips also rejected their audition tapes. Eventually, an up-and-coming record producer, George Martin, saw their talent and offered them a contract with a small studio called Parlophone, and the rest, as we say, is history. The Beatles went on to become legendary in pop music, and in my opinion the greatest band of all time, a catalyst and guiding influence for so many bands that followed them.

Fred Smith and the 'C' term paper

In the early 1970s, a young college student named Fred Smith wrote a term paper for his economics class at Yale University in the United States. He envisioned an overnight, nationwide delivery system for urgent packages. There was really nothing like it in the US in those days, or for that matter anywhere else in the world. However, his professor did not feel his idea was well-thought-out and gave him a C on his paper.

But that term paper planted a seed for Fred Smith, and he was not going to be deterred by his professor or by anyone else. He took the ideas from his paper and created what is now one of the world's greatest companies: Federal Express, or FedEx as it has come to be known worldwide, with its distinguishing colors and logo. We see its packages, trucks, labels, pick-up boxes, even its planes, everywhere we go, it seems, even at the movies!

Today, Federal Express is revered as one of the best companies to work for anywhere in the world and has a significant percentage of the air express market both in the US and the rest of the world.

On August 27, 2001, the US postal service awarded FedEx the biggest contract deal in their history: a $7 BILLION contract to deliver three million pieces of mail every day.

Not bad for a guy who got a C—don't you think?

Believe in Your Ability to Succeed

Adversity is what introduces us to ourselves.
—George W. Bush

Always treat obstacles and challenges as new opportunities to learn and grow. Successful people do not let setbacks bother them or deter them in their desire to achieve.

I would like to share with you the stories of two people with incredible courage and belief in themselves. One you may know and the other you may not.

Natalie Du Toit

In the 2002 Commonwealth Games, Natalie Du Toit, an 18-year-old swimmer from Cape Town, South Africa, won Gold in the 50m and 100m disabled swimming events and broke two world records on the way. This is a remarkable feat in itself, but what really sets her apart and makes her story so remarkable and inspiring to us all, is that she also made it to the final round of the *able-bodied* 800-meter swimming event, where she swam a personal best time of 9 minutes, 13.57 seconds. Imagine making it to the final round, against outstanding able-bodied swimmers from all over the world, and competing in the event with only one leg! Amazingly, her story does not end there. She was also voted the top athlete of the 2002 Commonwealth Games. All 72 competing nations and territories of the Commonwealth voted for one athlete out of the many thousands who participated, and Natalie won with their unanimous decision. To add to her thrill, Natalie was also introduced to Queen Elizabeth as part of the 'special athletes' event.

An aspiring Olympic hopeful, Natalie tragically lost her left leg at the knee, in February 2001, as a result of a motorbike accident. However, her sheer determination had her back in the pool by May of that year, before she could even walk. To motivate herself, she made the Commonwealth Games a target, her point of focus. Her determination, dedication, courage and commitment drove her to success: she made the South African team for the 2002 games!

What impressed me so much about Natalie was what she said in her own words about her accident:

"I always imagined myself as the same person I was before the accident," and "I would love to get my leg back, but you have to get used to it not being there. I had it for 17 years of my life, but I have to get on without it."

A very special young lady, Natalie Du Toit is mature beyond her years and sets an example for all of us. Her star shines so brightly, and she has a heart, an attitude and a character we could all learn from. She is an inspiration for not only her teammates and her fellow South Africans but for people all over the world. Her situation makes some of our problems—mine, for sure—seem so trivial and small.

Christopher Reeve

In May 1995, Christopher Reeve, an American film star renowned for his role in the movie *Superman,* was a rider in the Commonwealth Dressage and Combined Training Association Horse Trials in Virginia, when his horse balked at a rail jump and pitched him forward where he landed, headfirst. His injuries, which were life-threatening, left the actor paralyzed from the neck down.

When Reeve regained consciousness, he found himself immobilized in a hospital bed and unable to breathe without the help of a machine to pump his lungs. His first reaction was to look into the eyes of his beloved wife, Dana, and say, "Maybe we should just let me go." In that critical moment, with the choice of life or death in the balance, she unhesitatingly responded, "You're still you, and I love you."

Since the accident, Christopher Reeve has become an activist for people with spinal cord injuries, raising millions of dollars for research to find a cure, and bringing awareness to the public at large.

He chooses to have an incredibly positive attitude and belief in himself and in life. The doctors have told him he will never walk again. His response is, "It's not a matter of IF I will walk again, it is just a matter of WHEN and HOW."

One wonderful story I heard about Reeve comes from the time of his initial recovery in hospital. He received thousands of cards, messages and gifts from people from all over the world. One stood out from the rest: It was a large, framed picture of the first successful Apollo Shuttle Mission to the moon. All the astronauts and mission crew had signed the picture; underneath were the words: "To Christopher, We found that nothing is impossible."

Christopher Reeve is an example of courage and inspiration, a true hero to so many people around the world. He chooses to see his challenges and obstacles not as excuses for failure but as reasons for success. He is also brave enough to show his vulnerability, which makes him even more real to so many people.

I've come to learn that all my past failures and frustrations were actually laying the foundation for the understandings that have created the new level of living that I enjoy today.
—Anthony Robbins, motivational guru

The one thing you must have is BELIEF in yourself. If you do not believe in your heart and mind that you can overcome your personal obstacles and challenges that you are facing now and that you will continue to face in your life, success will not come to you. You will never live up to your highest potential; you will always be a spectator on the sidelines of life, instead of a participant and a winning player.

If you believe you can, you probably can. If you believe that you won't, you most assuredly won't. Belief is the ignition switch that gets you off the launching pad.
—Denis Waitley, author of *The Psychology of Winning*

Ask yourself three critical questions

1. What factors are holding you back right now in your life?

2. What do you have to do RIGHT NOW to translate these factors into confidence and belief?

3. Do you truly believe that you can achieve your goals?

Turn Your Setbacks Into Opportunities

*To be challenged in life is inevitable; to be defeated is
optional.*
—Roger Crawford, author of *How High Can You Bounce?*

The one lesson I've clearly grasped in life is that there are always going to
be setbacks and disappointments. There are always going to be people who
promise us things and disappoint us. Maybe it is someone in a personal or a
business relationship that lets you down. Maybe it is a person you thought
was a friend who betrays you. Maybe it is someone who did not live up to
your expectations in a crunch, or maybe it is the prospective client who
promised you that big sale or contract and then let you down at the last
minute. These are not pleasant situations, but they are a fact of life. The
one thing I have learned from observing and studying people who are successful is to GET OVER IT!!

Successful people put the bad times or the setbacks down to a learning
experience. They also have the ability to forgive people who have let
them down, even their enemies, let go of unpleasant things that may
have happened to them in the past, and move forward to the future.
But as John F. Kennedy said, "Forgive your enemies, but never forget
their names."

It is not always pleasant when someone lets us down. Like most of you I
am sure, I have at some time experienced frustration, disappointment and,
yes, heartache.

SIX ways to turn setbacks into opportunities

1. Realize that life is not always easy or fair, and that things are not going
    to go your way 100 percent of the time. Be flexible and realistic in your
    expectations of others. This way you will not be disappointed if some-
    one does not deliver or live up to your expectations.

2. Be of the mindset that setbacks are only temporary. Treat setbacks as feedback, nothing more and nothing less. Learn from them. Don't take everything personally.

3. Analyze what went wrong, why that person did not come through for you, why that sale did not happen, why that personal relationship may have broken down. Don't be too hard on yourself, but be realistic. My personal opinion is that most things that happen to us are for a reason. You will learn and grow more from being honest and true to yourself than from anything else. Remember that you can fool some of the people some of the time. I believe *most* of us can fool *most* of the people *most* of the time, but the one person we cannot fool, if we look honestly in that mirror, is OURSELF.

4. Remember the stories you have read, seen or heard about that have shown you that ordinary people can do extraordinary things when challenged. When your back is against the wall, the power of the human spirit and will is on your side if you believe in yourself and are prepared to dig deep and use the power that you possess.

5. Take each day as it comes. It is my opinion that, while this may be a worn cliché, these are valuable words. Expect less of other people and more of yourself. Don't take life and the people in your life so seriously. We all have our shortcomings.

6. Pick up a good book or watch a movie about someone you admire, someone who has overcome adversity, tragedy, failure or heartache. It will enrich your life, inspire you, and give you one or two nuggets of gold to take away and relate to your own life. The world is full of great stories.

In my life, many things have happened that have not been pleasant. When I have had the strength, resolve and courage to see those setbacks as learning experiences, I have turned many of them into opportunities. Don't give up easily when things go wrong. Misfortune and even tragedies happen, yet even these sometimes have a silver lining for those of us who believe in ourselves. Never underestimate your resolve, and always listen to your heart—it will not lie to you.

Be Willing to Sacrifice and to Pay the Price

The truth of the matter is that you always know the right thing to do. The hard part is doing it.
—General H. Norman Schwarzkopf,
Retired US Army General

Realize that whatever you want to do or achieve in your life, there is going to be a price to pay, or some sacrifice you will have to make. Where I grew up in Manchester, in Northern England, there is a slang expression: "You get naught for naught in this world." In other words, you get nothing for nothing, and anybody who thinks life is easy should think again. If there were no price to pay, we would all have that supposedly 'easy life.' We could lose weight at a whim, get fit instantly, study for that degree in our spare time, and make lots of money. Oh, if it were all that simple!

We all know from our own experiences that in the real world very few things come easily. I know in my life, when I wanted to take control of my speech, there was a tremendous price I had to pay, involving sacrifice, internal pain and hard work. If you really want something badly enough, I truly believe that you can achieve it, but first you must be willing to step out of your comfort zone.

Exercise: FIVE changes I would like to make in my life and am willing to pay the price for

Reflect for a few minutes on what sacrifices you have made in the past, what has worked for you, and what has not worked for you. Now, jot down five changes you want to make in your life, and beside them write: "I am willing to pay the price because I feel this is very important to do." This becomes a statement of commitment.

1. _____
2. _____
3. _____

4. _____

5. _____

Don't Take Life So Seriously

Richard Carlson, in his wonderful book *Don't Sweat the Small Stuff...and It's All Small Stuff,* writes about the simple ways to keep the little things from taking over your life.

For many years I used to sweat the small stuff. In fact I used to worry about everything, blow things out of proportion, make a big deal out of the smallest thing. Does this sound familiar to you? Do I detect a little chuckle or smile as you think of your own situation?

When I started to learn how to control my speech, I also learned how to not take life so seriously. I incorporated these lessons into my daily life, and they helped me to calm down and, I hope, become a better and more tolerant person. Most importantly, these thoughts gave me a certain peace of mind. Let me share them with you.

- You do not always have to be right in everything you do; you do not have to have all the answers. It is okay to make a mistake; it is okay not to have the last word or the last laugh. Learn to let go.

- Give other people credit for some of the good things that happen to you. Many people are going to help you along the way. Give them credit as a way to let them know how much you care about them, how much they mean to you.

- Don't take today so seriously—tomorrow is another day. Think of all the great things that are going on in your life.

- Think before you speak. If you need a few seconds before you answer a question, then take them in order to be able to respond comfortably. One of the hardest things in life to take back is the spoken word.

Words are very powerful. They can make us feel great, and they can also bring us and other people down. Never underestimate the power of the spoken word.

- Try to give people in your life the benefit of the doubt. I know this is not easy sometimes, and it is still a habit I wrestle with, but be more tolerant of other people. You will be glad you are.

- Look at people from the perspective of how you can help them, instead of how they can help you. By following this one principle, you will make more friends than you can imagine.

- Learn to switch off and recharge at least once during the day. Mr. Bell, my speech teacher, taught me this. Take 5, 10 or 15 minutes out of your day, preferably at lunchtime, to just find a quiet corner and think. Make this your time. Maybe read some inspiring quotes or affirmations. Do some breathing or meditation exercises, whatever it is that relaxes you. This is a very simple but powerful time. It will re-energize you and set you up for the rest of the afternoon.

You Have Bigger Fish to Fry

Some people spend much of their time worrying about what other people think of them, trying to please other people, instead of trying to please themselves. Do you recognize those traits in yourself? For many years I was always trying to please other people, trying to fit in, not wanting people to think I was different because of my unusual way of speaking. I just wanted to be liked. I would go to extraordinary lengths to be one of the 'in crowd.' I always felt I was inferior to other people and that everybody looked down at me, and I spent too much of my time focused on these feelings.

What I did not realize for all those years is that if you do not respect your-self, you cannot expect other people to respect you. In my case, a lack of self-respect came from having low self-esteem, and a lack of confidence. Once I embraced confidence and a belief in myself, and took responsibility for my life by recognizing and doing something about my speech situation, I truly became a different person.

THREE principles that contribute to self-confidence

1. Respect yourself.

2. Respect others.

3. Take responsibility.

Exercise: Inspiration to action

What inspiration have you gained from this chapter and the stories of Natalie Du Toit and Christopher Reeve?

_____

_____

_____

What is the NUMBER ONE thing holding you back right now from achieving what you want in life?

_____

_____

_____

Do you see the opportunity or the obstacle? Do you see the glass half-empty or the glass half-full?

_____

_____

_____

What is stopping you RIGHT NOW from doing what you want?

_____

_____

_____

Take Full Responsibility for Success in Your Life

The price of greatness is responsibility.

—Winston Churchill

Successful People Take 100 Percent Responsibility for Their Actions

Responsibility is about taking action and being in control of our own situations. It is about becoming accountable to ourselves, and that means not blaming anybody else when things go wrong—and, from time to time, we all know that things will go wrong. Responsibility is not always an easy choice, but it is always the right choice.

There are, of course, many people who can help us along the way. We certainly can't—nor should we try to—do everything alone. Ultimately, however, no matter how much support or encouragement we have, each of us must take the first step up to the plate, even though sometimes the first step is the hardest.

There are two primary choices in life: to accept conditions as they are, or to accept the responsibility for changing them.
—Denis Waitley, author of *The Psychology of Winning*

Taking that 100 percent responsibility for our own destiny means that we cannot wait for someone else to come along and make all the magic happen. We cannot rely on anybody else to make our dreams come true. We cannot ask anybody else to wave the magician's wand and make everything okay. We have to be in control. Successful people know this.

- Successful people take decisive action.

- Successful people step up to the plate.

- Successful people do not rely on other people, but they do thank them for their contribution.

- Successful people lead.

- Successful people are the masters of their own ship.

- Successful people do not blame other people for their own shortcomings.

- Successful people do what is necessary in order to achieve.

- Successful people unequivocally, absolutely, take 100 percent responsibility for their personal and professional choices and decisions.

Champions take responsibility. When the ball comes over the net, you can be sure I want that ball.
—Billie Jean King, tennis legend

It took me a very long time to learn about the importance of taking responsibility. While I was confident in my professional life, I lacked self-assurance in my personal life, particularly when it came to my stuttering disability. In my professional life, I knew that to get ahead, I had to take charge and be responsible for my own advancement and success. As for the stuttering disability, for a long time I was not prepared to do what was necessary, to take a risk or maybe to inconvenience myself by doing all the hard work which I knew was going to be necessary to overcome my problem.

Ask yourself...

In what areas of my life do I need to take responsibility?

_____

_____

_____

What is stopping me from taking responsibility?

_____

_____

_____

Exercise: Take responsibility

There are so many ways to take control, to take responsibility. Read the following list, and check all the answers that apply to your own life.

I need to take responsibility for:

[ ]   going back to school and getting that degree

[ ]   my finances

[ ]   spending more time with my loved ones

[ ]   picking up the phone and calling old and new clients

[ ]   volunteering and taking a leadership role in an association where I am a member

[ ]   eating healthy food

[ ] starting or restarting that exercise program

[ ] attaining my ideal weight

[ ] reading more

[ ] writing that book

Now make your own list.

I am going to take responsibility for:

1. _____
2. _____
3. _____
4. _____
5. _____
6. _____
7. _____
8. _____
9. _____
10. _____

As with meeting goals, taking responsibility means setting deadlines and determining a solid course of action. Successful people do not wait for or rely on others to create happy outcomes. They take responsibility for their conditions and circumstances, put themselves in the driver's seat, and steer in the direction of their own rewards.

Build Winning and Lasting Relationships

Successful people are always looking for opportunities to help other people. Unsuccessful people are always asking "What's in it for me? "

—Brian Tracy

Success Depends on Our Relationship Choices

I believe that in business and in life, a great deal of our success is related to the connections we make and the subsequent relationships we build with people. This includes family, friends, business partners and anyone we allow to have an impact on our lives. So many people do not understand the power of relationships. They think success is all about themselves. Oh, how wrong they are! If there is one thing I have learned in my life, both personally and professionally, it is that *success is about relationships*.

Those who think that relationships are built overnight are doomed to failure because relationships take time to nurture and build. Others have to like, trust and respect you before they will consider doing business with you. The expression "People do not care what you know until they know that you care" is a valuable one to remember.

Successful people realize that with every person they meet comes an opportunity to build a connection to the future. Short-sighted people focus on the sale, the transaction, the order, the short-term win. Smart people focus on the long term and on building a win-win relationship; they build relationships for the future, not just for today.

We live in a world where few of us have a product or service that nobody else has. We may think that what we have is the best, but the reality is that the competition thinks the same of their products. We also live in a world where everyone is looking for instant results, quick fixes or miracles; everyone is impatient for results, sales and numbers. Successful individuals are those who look to the long term in the relationships they are building, but focus on the shorter term for the value and results they can deliver to others.

Ways to build winning relationships with people

I am going to share with you some of the methods I've used over the years for building relationships. Many of them are certainly not unique to me, nor do I claim them as my own. Fortunately, I've had some very good mentors. They taught me well, and I thank them for sharing their valuable information with me. I have profited, as will you, by adding your own unique interpretation to what I've learned. Using the wisdom of successful people, and applying it to your own philosophy and behaviors, will set you apart.

Enter into a relationship to GIVE, not to GET. I have found that one of the best ways to build a connection and a long-term relationship is to ask how you can serve. For example, in sales, one of the recommended ways to grow your business is to network and ask for referrals. I have found that one of the best ways to build winning relationships in networking is by asking clients how you might be able to help them build *their* business. For example: "How would I recognize a good prospective client for you?" This has to be genuine and come from the heart, but people are so used to people wanting something from them, that this statement stands out. It creates a win-win situation and gets the relationship off to a good start in a non-threatening way. Who would not want you to help them? And aren't people more likely to help people who are good and kind to them first?

There is quite a distinction between selling and serving, particularly in the mind of the customer, but I believe that if you genuinely *try to serve your customer* instead of selling to them, the sale will take care of itself—every time. Remember the words of Zig Ziglar, best-selling author of *See You at the Top* and *Zig Ziglar's Secrets of Closing the Sale*: "Help enough people get what they want, and you will get what you want." I learned this first-hand when I was a sales consultant for Jobar Ltd. When I first started in my territory, my boss, Joe Scaglione, who taught me so much about service, sales and building relationships with people, said, "Just go out and make friends with people." It sounds so simple, but what Joe meant was that it takes time to build and nurture a relationship, and this is true no matter what business, profession or industry you are in. Learn to identify what *others*, not you, actually want or need.

Go out to make friends. With Nexxus, I had inherited a territory that was pretty rundown. I was taking over for a sales consultant who had not built a good reputation. He had not been dependable in the eyes of the salon owners, and they were not happy with the service they had received. In fact, many of them had discontinued the product. At first, sales went down even further. Since the hair salons didn't know me, they didn't trust me and, in an odd way, they felt betrayed that the other consultant had left. Luckily, another valuable lesson that I learned from Joe was to not take things personally, so I stayed focused. For the first few weeks, I was mainly just trying to 'put out fires' by doing everything Joe told me to do: take returns, show empathy, be kind and make friends. When I told them I would be back next week to take care of them, some of them just laughed and said, "Sure," but I kept showing up week after week. Most of the time I did not get an order, but I showed up anyway. Just by showing up, I was demonstrating that I was reliable and trustworthy. I always went in smiling and respectful of them, and most importantly, not looking at them in terms of what I could sell them, but in terms of how I could serve them.

Ultimately, I was able to turn the territory around, and in fact, I won several awards for sales growth and volume.

Seek out people you can learn from. Join associations and organizations that you are interested in, both on a personal and professional level. This step will put you in contact with like-minded people with whom you have something in common, and from whom you can learn your trade. I know we are all busy, but successful people make and find the time to 'join'—no question about it.

To give you an example: When I first made the decision to become a professional speaker, I made a very smart move by joining the Toronto chapter of the Canadian Association of Professional Speakers. I did not just join the association, but became actively involved in it, volunteering to do whatever was needed within my capability. Interestingly, although it wasn't my intention, I found that as soon as I did this, people started to take more notice of me. I found that I got to know people on a more personal level and made some important connections that allowed me to learn and to grow.

One of my jobs was helping our program chair by confirming the attendance of all the guest speakers we were bringing into our chapter, some of them quite famous and well experienced in the craft of professional speaking. As I contacted them, I began to build some personal relationships. I would offer my services, sometimes to help them sell the products they planned to bring for their program, sometimes picking them up at the airport and chauffeuring them around. They were very appreciative of my efforts, and as a result of those efforts, I have built wonderful relationships with a lot of people, and have learned and continue to learn much from them.

What groups would you like to get involved in both personally and professionally? How can you give back to those groups and contribute to them?

Find additional ways to distinguish yourself. If you are a person who hands out business cards, sorry, but neither your name nor your title is likely to make you memorable. You are going to have to find a way to make your card stand out. Use your imagination. For example, have your card made up as a CD-ROM—business card size. Many printing companies are producing these now. A card like that will certainly impress and stand out. At the very least, people will keep the card until they have had time to view the information on the CD.

Design a postcard and have it printed. Research shows that people are not likely to throw out a nice postcard that has something valuable on it. I have a postcard that I change every few months. It has a nice background, and there is a motivational or success quote, sometimes my own, sometimes someone else's, printed on it. My contact information is on the back of the card, but on the front, there is something of interest or value to the person receiving it. I often run into people who tell me that they still have my card posted in their office or on their fridge, sometimes a couple of years after we have met. And when they need a speaker, whose name do you think they will remember?

Do something original. People who are successful do the things other people do not do, and it only takes a little imagination. If you want to stand out, don't be a spectator. Be a player! Get out on the field! Enter the competition and be outstanding!

The key to successful networking is to stay in front of your target. You want to be top of someone's mind when they finally want or need what you have to offer. The postcard I have described is one way to put yourself there.

Another way to stand out is to have a newsletter. You can distribute it by mail, fax or e-mail. A successful newsletter must contain something of value and benefit to those who receive it. Nothing will upset and alienate your readers and get them to 'unsubscribe' as quickly as a newsletter that's merely a blatant 'infomercial' for your products or services.

A lesson In business cards

Have you ever been to a networking session and stayed behind until the end to talk to someone? Check out the waste paper bins on your way out in the hallways—they will be full of business cards. I am not saying you should not hand out your card, but the aim is to get other people's cards and then follow up.

Successful people know that getting the other person's business card gives you control of the situation. Without it, you are left waiting for someone to contact you, and chances are, unless you have something incredibly special to offer, that is unlikely to happen. The truth of the matter is that people lose or throw away business cards, and though they mean well enough when they accept your card, they will soon forget about you.

When you take someone's business card, it is protocol to take a moment to look at it and make a comment about it. I believe that doing this not only shows your respect for that person but also demonstrates that you are professional enough to take the time to consider the information offered to you. If you are going to write on it, and I think there are times when it is very appropriate to do so, it is important to ask permission. (There are cultures in which writing on a business card is considered rude.) I like to write things on the back of a card. It may just be something to familiarize me with that particular person, or it may be a reminder to do some follow-up. I have a poor memory sometimes, especially when I'm meeting lots of people. Sometimes adding a simple notation to someone's card can help me to remember them.

Once you have been given a card, you can determine someone's level of interest by asking for a convenient time for you to follow up. If the individual does not offer a business card or is reluctant to give you a name or information, forget about them. This person may be going through the motions but is not a good prospect for you. Don't hold your breath waiting for a call.

Truly successful people take responsibility for networking. This means that they seek out opportunities to make connections and keep the connections going. They commit notes to a daily log or diary about a date to touch base with people they have met and then actually make the connection. They ask permission to follow up again, and they keep making those connections with the people whose relationship they value.

Some concluding tips for building relationships

- Think long term.

- Make connections for the future.

- Ask yourself, "How can I help that other person?"

- Treat every person you meet with respect.

- Attend networking sessions and join associations that you are interested in.

- Get involved with the groups you join and take on a leadership role.

- Give other people referrals and introduce them to your network.

- Go the 'extra mile.'

- Help other people achieve what they want.

The Art of Networking

To pursue success effectively, you must build supportive relationships that will help you work toward your goals. To build those relationships, you need to trust others; and to earn their trust, you in turn must learn to be trustworthy.

—Stedman Graham, author of *You Can Make It Happen: A Nine-Step Plan for Success*

Make Contact

We have talked about the people you associate with and how they impact your success. In this chapter we look at the art of building a network of people who will contribute to your success.

To make new contacts, be they personal or business-related, you must first go to the right places. These are places where you are likely to find people who are interested in the same things you are, who are looking for the service or product you provide, or who can simply challenge you to try harder. Some of these great places include the following:

- your local Chamber of Commerce or Board of Trade;
- business networking groups;

- professional associations;
- non-profit groups;
- alumni organizations;
- groups such as Rotary and Kiwanis.

These are only a few of the possibilities. You need to look at each situation that puts you in contact with others as an opportunity to build new and valuable connections.

> *Opportunity is all around us, it knocks for those of us who have the eye trained to see it, the ear trained to hear it, the hand trained to grasp it, and the mind trained to use it.*
> —Kemmons Wilson, founder of Holiday Inn Hotels

Stay in Touch

We stay in touch with people by following up with them—sending postcards, telephoning them to find out how they are doing, sending them a newspaper or magazine article that would be of interest to them, just letting people know you are thinking of them. The article does not have to be business-related; find out what their hobbies and interests are away from the office. Opportunity often comes from being top of mind, and that means nurturing the relationships you are building by adding value to people's lives, and simply by showing that you care and are thinking of them.

Staying in touch involves DISCIPLINE. Discipline is diligently and relentlessly sending that handwritten note to your prospect, customer, client or new acquaintance. Discipline is working, updating and managing your database or contact management system at all times. Discipline is doing the things most people do not or will not do in order to be successful, to get that winning edge. People do business with people they trust, respect, like and, most importantly, know they can rely on—no matter what.

As I stated earlier, most successful business relationships are built over a period of time. Successful sales people take between six and eight calls, if not more, to close a sale. There are many people who give up after the first or second attempt. I can attest to that after spending many years in the sales world. The people who were most successful were the ones who were staying in touch, being diligent, doing little things consistently, and going about their business in a professional way, always with a smile and a positive attitude.

Exercise: How I stay in touch

List the *methods* you use to stay in touch with your customers, clients and prospects.

_____

_____

_____

Ask yourself...

What am I doing today to make sure my customers, clients and those I want to stay in touch with, do not have a chance to forget me tomorrow?

People will forget you if you do not stay in touch with them. Be imaginative and creative. You want to be top of mind when a buying decision is imminent. Call them in the bad times, when things are not going too well for them. They will remember you for it. Just make sure that you stay in touch! This one simple lesson in discipline will grow your business in so many ways.

Be Tenacious

A friend of mine, John, is an advertising sales representative for a group of newspaper companies. He sells advertising space and related services. Recently, he told me a story that I think shows the importance and payoff of tenacity.

For over two years, John diligently kept in touch with a certain prospect, an executive at a very large Fortune 500 company. John had asked permission and established a contact schedule with this person; thus, every six weeks, without fail, John kept in telephone contact (his prospect's preference), and every so often sent his prospect information in the mail.

For over two years (that's tenacity!), he kept in touch, getting no business from this person at all. Then, one day out of the blue, the prospect finally made a call to John, telling him that his company was undergoing a huge change of direction. It seems they not only wanted to do some major advertising in the newspapers that John represented, but they also needed consulting on the design and implementation of the whole campaign.

Had John let that relationship slip away, or had he not been as tenacious, he may have lost what turned out to be his biggest sale ever. *The total value of the project was worth well over one million dollars!*

Key points about keeping in touch

• Always respect people's time.

• Always ask permission to stay in touch and how. Never assume anything.

• Do as you say you will. People say, "under-promise and over-deliver," and I agree with that to a degree, but my philosophy has always been very simple: *Keep your promises.* Anything more is a bonus, but the most important thing is to be true to your word.

I have said this before, and I will say it many times: people do business with people they like, trust and respect. John asked his now Number One Client, once the contract was signed, why he thought of him after two years. His client answered, "I admired you for staying in touch with me for so long, for always being courteous and respectful, and for never being too pushy. In the end, there was no one, in my opinion, more deserving of the deal, and I knew that I could count on you for quality service, competitive pricing, and definitely for keeping in touch with me."

Exercise: Who needs my attention?

List the *people* you are neglecting to stay in touch with, or could reconnect with.

_____

_____

_____

_____

Check all of the statements below that apply to you:

[   ]   Do you give up too easily on your prospects?

[   ]   Do you let your ego get in the way of your success?

[   ]   Do you take rejection too personally?

[   ]   Do you take the answer "No" as a reason to give up?

If you are nodding your head to a number of these statements, you need to re-evaluate your relationship strategy and your overall approach to selling. If you answered "No" to all these questions, congratulations, you are in the top percent of sales people. You are doing all the right things with the right attitude and mindset.

Find an Advocate

An advocate is someone who genuinely likes, respects and trusts you. Advocates love your work and they want to help you. Treat these people as gold.

Bob Burg, author of *Endless Referrals* and *Winning Without Intimidation*, sums it up this way: "Does he or she like you, and trust you? Does he want you to succeed? Does she want to help you find new business? If so, then you have a 'Personal Walking Ambassador.'"

Exercise: Identifying your personal ambassadors

Who, in your life, are your advocates, your 'Personal Walking Ambassadors'?

_____

_____

_____

_____

How do you plan to stay in touch with these people?

_____

_____

_____

_____

Build those personal connections!

Having a plan to stay in touch may seem a little unnecessary, but it is the one sure way to stay visible to key people. Any successful business person will tell you that. There are great books about this, and each has its own theory. My rule of thumb is to keep in touch with these people at least once every 30 days, either by telephone, e-mail or through a letter or note. Send them something. It does not always have to be business-related, and in fact, sometimes it's better if it's not. Just a friendly "I was just wondering how you were doing" will suffice. Call it small talk, but I think people appreciate that you're not always talking shop. Take an interest in them. Get to know them. Find out what you have in common with them outside of business. Do not see people only as business transactions.

Many business people do not take the time to do this, but remember the golden rule: treat people as you would like to be treated. Make the people in your life feel special, important and great. If you do that, they will enrich your life and open up doors for you in ways you could not even imagine.

Link Your Networking Strategy to Your Personal Success Definition

In Chapter 1, you described your own definition of success. Your network and your approach to networking, following up and staying in touch, all need to be aligned with this definition.

We choose to be successful in business and in life the moment we decide not to settle for mediocrity, the moment we are prepared to step out of our comfort zone, and do whatever it takes to reach our goals.

The key is to realize that success does not drop on your doorstep. Be prepared to go after the success you desire, to create a game plan and complete the plays. You may not always get the breaks you feel you deserve, but with vision, courage, responsibility and commitment, by doing the things most people choose not to do, and by getting out of your comfort zone, you *can* create that life you desire.

Most people dream about success, but truly visionary thinkers envision, create and go after the success they want.

Success is not a spectator sport. One of the key plays to being successful is to diligently keep in touch with people, to not have an attitude of WIIFM (What's in it for me) but to be constantly thinking of what you can be doing for them. Have that attitude and you will go far in life.

> *Whatever you want to do, do it, because*
> *the impossible is just the untried.*

Create and Form Win-Win Alliances With People

When I opened my first hairdressing salon, many years ago at the tender age of 21, in my home city of Manchester, England, I thought I knew it all. I should have listened to the words of former US college basketball coach John Wooden who said, "It's what you learn after you think you know it all that really matters." There were certainly many areas of my business that I was really naïve about back then, but the art of creating win-win alliances with people was, fortunately, not one of them. I learned this first-hand from my father as I was growing up, by observing and helping him after school and on weekends in his butcher shop. He was a master of building alliances in his modest but successful business. He knew every other merchant in his area. They referred business to him regularly, and he did likewise for them. He treated all his customers with the same level of courtesy, regardless of who they were or how much they spent. Each, in turn, referred all their friends to him. My dad was a master butcher and proud of it, and he let it show. He was also a master in customer service. Maybe I am a little biased, but I believe these two traits made him one of the best alliance builders I have ever seen. He taught me a lot about building relationships and how to treat people. His words of wisdom to me were: "Be in business for your customers, and your customers will be in business for you."

What I did with this knowledge, in my hair salons, later as a sales professional, and even now in my professional speaking business, was to adhere to the following two key principles. They may be of help to you in your business as well.

1. Find out your customers' or clients' needs and wants, and then find a way to deliver them. Sometimes, this means referring the business away from yourself. As an example: there are times as a professional speaker when I get asked by a client to speak about something that is not within my area of expertise, and as a professional, I politely explain this to my client. However, with their permission, I recommend one of my professional colleagues who, I feel, would be perfect for a particular topic or event. This creates a win-win situation for me and my client: for me, because I maintain integrity with my client, and for them, because their requirements are satisfied. I save them the time and hassle of having to look for someone else, and I become a trusted resource for them. In addition, I build networking relationships with my professional speaking colleagues who will also win by securing new bookings.

    Similarly, when I was a sales professional, I often directed my clients to an appropriate source for a product or service that I thought was a good fit for them—even though that source may have been one of my competitors. In my retail business as a hair salon owner, I teamed up with other merchants in the village where my store was located. We promoted each other's businesses and became advocates for each other. Word-of-mouth or referral business beats advertising any day.

This links to the second principle:

2. Know what you are good at and be the best at it. Don't apologize for what you are not.

Exercise: Building your networking strategy

What am I really good at?

_____

_____

_____

_____

Who can I help to move his/her business forward, and at the same time, better serve my clients/customers?

_____

_____

_____

_____

Who can I form a strategic alliance with that will create a win-win situation for both of us?

_____

_____

_____

_____

Remember that to become a trusted advisor, resource and friend, you must help people, and not because of what you can get in return, or for the rewards that may come your way. Help people because you genuinely want to. If life teaches us anything, it is that good things do happen to good people. People remember those who have helped them along the way.

Communication: Your Greatest Asset

Learn to Be a Great Listener

You will make more friends in two months by being interested in other people than you will in two years by trying to get people interested in you.

—Dale Carnegie

Most people enjoy talking about themselves and what they are doing. It's human nature, and there is nothing wrong with that as long as someone does not monopolize a conversation. I am sure we have all experienced situations—I know I have—where a person has gone on and on about his or her own agenda, hardly allowing others to get a word in. Think about a time when you have been in a similar situation. How did you feel toward that person? I anticipate that your response was not very positive. Not only is it disrespectful and boring for someone to go on about himself or herself constantly, but it also gives the impression to others that he or she is not really interested in the other person and is only self-centered. To become truly interesting to people, you must be interested in them first.

Successful people spend more time listening and asking questions than talking. They are not focused on finding that break in the conversation that will enable them to steer it around to themselves and their issue or point of view. My rule of thumb is to talk 20 percent of the time and listen intently for 80 percent of the time.

Listening is a skill that most of us could improve upon. In my opinion, it is certainly a secret weapon, and with practice and discipline, it is something we can perfect. A good listener is smart enough to know that the more one listens, the more one learns. In the business world, it is my observation that the most successful people are not necessarily the best talkers, but are certainly the best listeners. They are the people who ask questions of their customers and clients, the ones who take a genuine interest in other people. Good listeners maintain eye contact; I find it insulting to speak to someone whose eyes stray all over the place, because their unspoken message to me is that they are totally disinterested in what I am saying and that I'm merely a distraction or interruption to something more important. A good listener is always popular, and this does not just apply to the business world, but to personal relationships and social settings as well. Being a good listener will always make you welcome.

One of my guidelines for effective listening is to ask three questions of the person I am having a conversation with before I start to talk. I also always try to finish off the conversation by letting the other person have the last word. Try it and see how it works for you.

As a result of my severe stuttering disability, I was very shy and reserved as a teenager, and of course, I did not speak very well. In fact, sometimes I went for long periods where I could hardly speak at all. The words would just not come out, and if they did, I would be twisting and straining my face and body trying to get the words formed, so I would frequently retreat into silence as the easy way out.

At the age of 17, I went for a job interview at a hairdressing salon. As you can imagine, because of my speech, my track record at job interviews was not good. You know the scenario: the person conducting the interview closes with a smile and says something like, "Thank you for coming, we will be in touch." Well, in my case, they were never in touch.

One particular interview was a little different. Neil, the manager, scanned my resume for a minute or two, and then, instead of asking me questions, he started telling me about himself. In fact, he never stopped talking about himself for the 20 minutes the interview lasted. This suited me fine, as I could not speak well and didn't want to leave a bad impression by talking much anyway, but I learned a valuable lesson that day in that hairdressing salon in Manchester, England. I learned that by smiling, showing interest, nodding occasionally, by asking simple questions and by not doing all the talking, you could make a strong impression. Neil certainly responded to this—I got hired for the job. After I had been turned down so many times before, that interview certainly made a lasting impression on me. I have never forgotten it.

I never realized in the years that I stuttered severely that I was actually gaining a unique skill that would serve me well both then and now. Stuttering actually helped me to hone my listening skills.

Ask yourself...

How good a listener am I?
Do I truly listen to people when they speak to me?
Do I give people my undivided attention?
Do I show empathy?

Tips for good listening

- Be interested in other people always. Let the other person talk three times more than you do. Try to ask questions and listen to the answers 80 percent of the time, and speak for only 20 percent of the time.

- When someone is speaking to you and is just about to finish off a viewpoint and you think it is your turn to respond, RESIST THAT TEMPTATION. Ask that person one more question. This shows genuine interest in them, and you would not believe how much people will appreciate this one simple action. Try it, and see how effective it will make your conversations and the difference it will make in how people view you.

- Always give people your full attention. One of the greatest gifts we can give people is the true gift of our attention.

- Sometimes the words we leave unsaid are the smartest words of all.

One of our foremost means of communications is conversation. Asking good open-ended questions and then listening to the answers creates conversation. I read an interesting statistic recently: It takes only 15 percent of the human brain to take in something we hear. That leaves 85 percent of the brain to truly appreciate what's being said.

In my communication workshops, I conduct an exercise in which I pair two people and ask one of them to be the listener for 90 seconds, and the other to talk about something he or she is passionate about. The results of this short exercise are very interesting. The feedback I get from the listeners is that 90 seconds seems like an eternity. It is very hard for them to keep quiet and not try to cut in with their own thoughts. The speakers, on the other hand, say they enjoy the experience immensely and that 90 seconds goes by too fast.

Try this exercise with a family member, a friend or a colleague at work. Practice the role of the listener. You will acquire a skill that will definitely give you an advantage over your competition. It will help you develop better relationships in your personal life as well as your professional one. When you come home from work, make a point of asking your spouse or significant other about his or her day first, and resist the urge to jump right in with details about your day.

Here is another interesting fact: I have never seen anyone close a sale, complete a transaction, negotiate a contract or get the prospective customer or client to sign on the dotted line *while they were still doing the talking*.

We cannot not communicate. Everything we do or say, or don't do and say, sends out a strong message to other people.
—John Woods, editor and publisher

Speak the Language of Your Audience

I have learned over the years (through personal experience and from observing smart, successful people) to speak to people I would like to do business with, or connect with in some way, *at their own level*. What I mean by that is this: If the person I am communicating with is speaking slowly, I should slow down my pace. Similarly, if this person speaks faster than I normally speak, I try to quicken my pace to match. This is not always easy or comfortable, but I have found it to be very effective and have heard the same observations from quite a few people.

The same respect for your listener applies to your choice of words. Have you ever been at a presentation where the speaker was obviously highly educated and chose to demonstrate this with a higher level of vocabulary? I certainly have, and I have to say that I wasn't impressed; in fact, I was downright frustrated by the jargon. Successful people adapt their language to the level of the listener. If they are speaking to academic peers, fancy words work. Otherwise, standard vocabulary is more appropriate for most listeners.

Use Non-Verbal Communication

Being a great communicator also means communicating non-verbally. In fact, it is our non-verbal communication that accounts for the greater part of people's impressions of us, both in business and personal relationships. There is research that shows that only seven percent of the impact of our communication is derived from the words we use, while 38 percent of that impact is based on tone—be it friendly, sarcastic, enthusiastic, happy or threatening. And most interestingly, in face-to-face communication, body language conveys 55 percent of our messages. Body language includes facial expressions, gestures and movement. To me, this seems a staggering statistic. It certainly tells me that words are not as important as we think, but it also tells me that we need to choose our words well.

I can't express strongly enough the power of little things, such as a smile. A smile costs nothing, but means everything. It can light up a room and show you are non-threatening. It can break those awkward moments, and show people your intentions. It is truly one of the most powerful communication tools we have at our disposal.

Don't think smiling applies only when you are meeting people face to face. Get into the habit of smiling even if you are speaking on the telephone. Believe me, your listener can hear a smile in your voice. I often smile into the telephone receiver; I believe it prepares me for friendly communication and puts me in a better frame of mind. In truth, I think the world would be a much better place if we all lightened up a bit more and did not take ourselves so seriously. A smile is a starting point.

Actions Do Speak Louder Than Words

How others perceive us involves a lot more than simply the words we use and our tone and body language. I believe that people may forget what you said to them, they may even forget what you did for them, but they will NEVER forget how you made them *feel*. Were you attentive? Were you passionate about what you were saying? Did you show an interest in what *they* were saying?

I feel that too many people are neglecting the personal touches found in a kind word or a sincere compliment. We live in a fast-paced world, and with all the technology available, many of us have forgotten the effect that a handwritten card or a quick phone call to say thanks can have. Successful people don't forget the little things.

Exercise: Communication audit

Ask yourself the following questions:

• Do I present an image of confidence when I meet people?

- Do I maintain eye contact with people at all times, or am I looking around at other things?

- Is my posture and body language reflecting that I am a person of confidence and success?

- Is my tone of voice consistent with the person I am talking to?

- Do I give the person I am communicating with my full attention? Be brutally honest with yourself about this one. If you can honestly say you do, I commend you for it, as I have personally found that most people do not.

- Do I pay attention to the little things?

- Do I smile enough?

Always be consistent in your communication and adhere to the principles above. You cannot, in my opinion, switch them on and off.

Speaking in Public

I couldn't deliver a speech to save my life. Before reading my first speech in front of a few hundred GE executives in Cooperstown, NY, I twice had to leave the front row of the auditorium to run to the bathroom.
> —Jack Welch, former CEO of General Electric
> and author of *Jack: Straight From the Gut*

Speaking in public is widely acknowledged as the number one social fear in the world. Some people say they would rather die than stand up in front of an audience. That may sound a bit extreme, but public speaking is a major fear and concern to a lot of people, and many go to great lengths to avoid it.

Speaking in public can mean anything from having to give a sales presentation at a meeting or to a prospective client, to having to introduce yourself or make an introduction at a social or business function in front of a group. It can mean having to give a speech at a wedding or happy gathering, or a eulogy at the funeral of a loved one or close friend.

Many of of you may still be thinking, "That is fine, but I never find myself in a public speaking situation." But as my professional colleague Patricia Fripp said, "All speaking outside of the privacy of your own home is public speaking."

SIX key points for keeping on track when speaking in public

1. Know your audience.
   Whenever possible, find out as much as you can about your audience. The more you know about their interests, challenges, concerns and motivations, the more prepared you will be for what may come up. When in doubt, be prepared for anything.

2. Capture their attention immediately.
   The first 60 seconds and the last 60 seconds are going to have the greatest impact on the success of your presentation, so come out punching, grab their attention, and close with a call to action.

3. Have a structure or approach to what you are saying.
   Nothing is going to lose the attention of your audience more quickly than rambling on aimlessly. Make sure that what you are saying flows and has a structure to it, so that people can understand what you are trying to tell them.
   Take time to plan out what you are going to say. Wherever possible, link your point to your audience's motivations and interests.

4. Apply the rules of non-verbal communication.
   I believe that effective communication is 20 percent *what* you know, and 80 percent *the passion you feel about* what you know. Passion is evident in your tone of voice, in your enthusiasm, and in your body

language. To repeat: people will forget a lot of what you tell them, but they will never forget how you made them feel in their heart.

5. Remember your goal.
    Your objective is likely to be one or more of the following:
    - to inform and educate;
    - to connect emotionally as well as intellectually;
    - to inspire;
    - to entertain;
    - to call to action.

    As you speak, remember which of these you are trying to accomplish and adjust your style accordingly.

6. Keep the three C's sacred.
    - Speak with **clarity**, so that people can understand your message.
    - Speak with **conviction**, so that people believe your message.
    - Speak with **confidence**, so people feel inspired and moved to action by your message.

Find opportunities to practice speaking

If you are in a situation where you are going to be required to speak in public and are trying to get over the fear of it, my recommendation is to seek out opportunities to practice.

Toastmasters International is the largest organization in the world for people who want to learn and practice the skills, craft and disciplines associated with effective public speaking. It teaches these in a non-threatening atmosphere of like-minded people.

I can't say enough about Toastmasters. It is a wonderful organization that has helped so many people who are nervous, fearful or uncomfortable about standing up and speaking before a crowd. It also has a great magazine, with lots of articles and tips about speaking, which is mailed to members on a monthly basis.

You can find out more about Toastmasters International by going to their website at www.toastmasters.org or by writing to them at:

Toastmasters International
P.O. Box 9052
Mission Viego, California
92690, USA

A few words about computer visuals

The computer is a wonderful tool if used correctly and effectively. In pre-sentations, there are computerized programs available for visually enhancing what you are saying, complete with colorful diagrams and sound. However, too many people use them as a crutch, or hide behind them. Think about the topic you are trying to present. Would it be of value to your listener to have a visual support to make your point? If so, then use it by all means, but remember that *you* are your most valuable visual aid. Never mind the bells and whistles, the graphics and music, and all the fancy technology that is available today to add to our presentations. People want to hear the facts, but they also want to see and hear the presenter, front and center stage. While the visual aids are interesting and can increase retention, people do not want a slick presentation if the presenter hides behind it.

One of my corporate clients recently did an experiment. The organization directed 150 of its executives across North America and Europe, who gave regular presentations, to reduce their dependence on computer-generated visual aids, and then, in some cases, *to stop using them* altogether. Audiences were solicited for feedback and the results were quite fascinating. A whopping 92 percent of those surveyed said they preferred the presenter alone. Some listeners commented that they felt the presenter seemed "more real," while many said that they felt the presenter spoke with more passion and enthusiasm.

If you are going to use visual aids, here is my rule of thumb: I liken it to packing to go on vacation. I pack a full suitcase of things I think I am going to need, then my wife removes 50 percent of what I have packed, and I still find I've taken along too much. With slides, for instance, use one out of every three. That will usually be sufficient to convey your message effectively, leaving *you* clearly in center stage. Less is always more! People can observe only so much in a presentation.

• • •

Create a great first impression with everyone you come into contact with. They say you never get a second chance to make a first impression, and I agree wholeheartedly. It is unfortunate, but people do judge us and sometimes too quickly. People can make a judgment about us within the first 20 seconds of meeting us: whether they like us, want to get to know us better, form a relationship with us or want to do business with us. I know about making great first impressions. Because of my severe stuttering, I *always* made a memorable first impression, but unfortunately, for all the wrong reasons!

People do judge us every day, whether we have a disability or not.

Invest in Your Personal and Professional Development

*Nurture your mind with great thoughts, for you will go no
higher than you think.*

—Benjamin Disraeli, British statesman

Successful people are naturally curious. Their thirst for information sets
them apart from others: they never stop learning; they develop new skills;
they are open to new ideas; they read books; they invest in tapes; they go
to seminars; and they subscribe to magazines and newsletters that help
them develop as individuals and professionals. In effect, they are information sponges, fueling their ambitions with knowledge.

Carve Out Time to Read

I did not invest very much time in my personal or professional development
until later in life. I now regret this. Unfortunately, I can't turn back the
clock; however, I can make up for lost time, and I certainly try my best to
do so. My personal strategy is to devote at least one hour a day to reading,
and whenever possible, I do more, most often when I am traveling. I read

the local and national daily newspapers to keep abreast of what is happening in the world and in the locale I am visiting. I read books. I listen to lots of tapes. I also find that with the Internet I have a constant wealth of knowledge and information at my fingertips.

If you want to be more successful in any aspect of your life, spend a few hours in your favorite bookstore or library, or seek out books in your travels. I spend a lot of time at airports and always look forward to visiting their bookstores.

If you can't spare a few hours, and I realize that may be unrealistic for a lot of people, go during your lunch hour or on a weekend. Please don't tell me that you don't have the time! When you really want to do something, and it is important to you, somehow you make the time. Charles Tremendous Jones, author of *Life Is Tremendous,* said, "Five years from now you will be the same person you are today. The only things that will separate you are the people you meet and the books that you read."

Books are one of the hidden secrets to success. Think about it—where else can you get incredible information from the greatest experts and most successful minds in history on basically any topic that is important and of interest to you? On every page, they share with you their philosophies, principles, mindsets and methods on anything—business, leadership, developing relationships, achieving happiness, reducing stress, being a better parent or spouse, or handling your finances. There is nothing you can't learn if you take the time to read. The knowledge that you can gain is incredible and it is available anytime, to anyone.

I personally find it very therapeutic to walk around bookstores. My collection of books and tapes represents one of the greatest investments I have ever made in my personal and professional development, and it is never too late to begin one.

Exercise: Satisfying curiosity

What one topic have you been curious about? What burning question do you have that you haven't found an answer to?

_____

_____

_____

_____

Take your question to your local bookstore or library and do a search. No doubt you'll find a helpful book that gives you the knowledge or answer you need.

Don't hesitate to visit any bookstore—soon. You'll be glad you did.

Join the 7 percent club

Did you know that, on average, only 7 percent of people in North America own a library card? That, to me, is both astounding and sad. For some people, constantly buying books and tapes may be unrealistic or beyond their budget; however, owning a library card is possible for anyone for a very modest charge, if not for free.

My wife and I made a point of taking our son Daniel to the library at the tender age of two. We would take him into the children's section and let him select two books each time. Many times he didn't have a clue what he was choosing, but I believe an independent thirst for knowledge was being engrained in him which, even at that age, was invaluable. Now, at age four, he has his own library card, and one of his favorite weekly outings is to accompany us to the local library.

Visit your local library. Take your family and make it an outing. Borrow the wonderful books and learning resources available through every lender. Take advantage of their additional resources offered in newspapers and magazines from all over the world.

Don't forget to befriend the librarians. They can guide you to information that would otherwise be difficult to find. I personally do a lot of research at the library and I treat my favorite librarian like gold. With her help and guidance, I have been able to locate key information—in half the time it would have taken searching on my own—that I might otherwise have missed. Discover one of the best-kept secrets in town—your library.

Exercise: Become a 7 percent club member

- Go to your calendar.

- Target the next available two-hour block.

- Schedule in a trip to the library.

- If you are going to make it a family trip, book it into their schedules.

- Make an investment in your personal and professional development. Borrow at least one book every time you visit and, more importantly, make sure you read it.

Use the Web, but use it wisely

The Internet and the World Wide Web are among the greatest inventions of the modern age. They put information at the fingertips of many people who might not otherwise have access to it. Just punch in a keyword for the topic you want to research, and see what comes up. The real challenge is sifting through the information and honing your search to find exactly what you are looking for. The task can become monumental.

To get good results from a Web search, you need a plan for what you want to research or view on the Internet; without one, you can end up surfing from site to site to site, and achieving little. Give yourself a time limit and stick to it.

Take Advantage of "Lost" Time to Learn

I don't know about you, but I lose a lot of time traveling to and from work, to and from appointments, and so on. However, I have learned to transform this time from "lost" to "found." I use it to listen to motivational tapes or books-on-tape. I receive some of these through subscriptions, but they are also readily available in bookstores and now even in many libraries. My wife used to drive frequently between Montreal and Toronto—a five-and-a-half-hour trip. On several occasions, upon her return, I would find her sitting in the driveway for an extended period of time before she came into the house, because she was listening to the end of a book-on-tape! With two small children, she found that this was a convenient way for her to invest in her own learning!

Exercise: Make a commitment

Ask yourself the following questions:

* When was the last time you read a book (this can be a novel or a book related to your profession or business) or listened to a motivational or professional tape?

_____

_____

* If you could find the time, what topic would you like to learn more about?

_____

_____

_____

- How much time will you invest in your development? Check the box
  that suits your lifestyle, but make this commitment!

I will devote:
- [   ]   30 minutes a day to my development
- [   ]   60 minutes a day to my development
- [   ]   120 minutes a day to my development
- [   ]   240 minutes a day to my development

You can break the time up to suit your schedule. It does not have to be taken all in one chunk. Block the time in your calendar for the next two weeks.

You may want to consider taking a speed-reading course. There are many available, and although I personally have not taken one, I have heard from many people that they are excellent.

My words of wisdom

Whatever area in your life it is that you wish to develop, do yourself a favor and make that investment in your growth and future TODAY. Devote a minimum of 30 minutes a day to your development. That is not too much time to carve out of your busy day. Be creative—there are no excuses if you really want to find the time!

Let Go of Perfection and Strive for Excellence

There is a big difference between perfection and excellence. Perfection is never wanting to make a mistake. Excellence is having the ability and the courage to want to learn from one's mistakes. Never confuse the two of them.

Stop Waiting for the Perfect Moment

One of the hardest lessons I learned while struggling with my speech was that it was okay to make mistakes. If I had not learned that lesson, I might never have conquered my stutter. The fear of failure would have been too much to overcome.

If you wait for that perfect moment to do something you have always wanted to do in your life or to make that necessary change, then you will never do it, because the truth of the matter is that there is no 'right' time. Truly, there may never be that 'perfect' moment, and waiting for it becomes another form of indecision and procrastination.

For years, I kept waiting for that right time to do something about my speech. Waiting for the perfect moment was much easier than facing my challenge head-on and taking responsibility. I did not want to fail, or even worse, make a mistake. I have since learned that successful people are courageous and are willing to make mistakes in order to learn from them. Successful people are willing to take risks and put themselves on the line. They readily let go of perfection, which is a fool's game, but never for one moment do they ever let go of *excellence*.

By nature, we tend to focus all our energies on our mistakes, our imperfections, and our reluctance to do things. On the other hand, if we can focus on our successes and what we are good at, we are set for action. Sometimes, we need to cut ourselves a bit of slack, and give ourselves a pat on the back. It's healthy and important to recognize that it is okay to make mistakes and not be perfect all the time.

In 1986, when I returned to my home in England from my speech course in Scotland, I had to take risks and open myself up for failure in order to continue my progress and to be successful with my speech endeavors. Everyday I had to push myself to try new things, to put myself in speaking situations that in the past would have been a nightmare for me and sometimes had been virtually impossible. In the past, my attitude was "if I can't do this perfectly, then I will not do it at all." My speech course taught me to let go of perfection, and I was then able to focus on the 90 percent of times that I achieved my speech goals for that particular day, and not on the 10 percent when I stumbled or when things went wrong. I am not saying that you should dismiss your mistakes or ignore what went wrong, just don't deny yourself the joy of your accomplishments. Savor the small victories in your life and always be willing to learn from your defeats and setbacks. Develop and use these as opportunities to set new and better habits to avoid making the same mistakes again.

Ask yourself...

- Do I allow myself a break now and again, or am I too hard on myself, always waiting for just that right moment to do something that is important to me?

- Do I focus on my accomplishments or do I waste energy by focusing on my mistakes and shortcomings?

- Do I take the time to analyze my mistakes and learn from them?

Exercise: Self-improvement goals

What are the five areas of your life that you wish to improve, but have not dealt with in the past because you were waiting for just the right time?

1. _____
2. _____
3. _____
4. _____
5. _____

Remember: Don't be so hard on yourself. Focus on the things you can control. Celebrate the fact that you tried. Realize that mistakes will happen in your life and that they are inevitable. Learn from those experiences, get over them, and then move on. Successful people have the ability to do that. There is no shame in losing, as long as you don't lose the lesson it teaches you.

Success and failure come in pairs; either you have a pair of aces called resolve and resilience, or a pair of jokers called wishing and wanting...it's your hand to play!
—Doug Firebaugh

Be Willing to Laugh at Yourself

Have you ever had a bad day?

In business and in life, we are all going to have bad days, days when things go wrong. Highly successful people have bad days too. The difference is that they have the ability to still make those bad days positive. They find the strength and resolve to dig down deep and show resilience. They see failure and disappointment as just part of the package and, in fact, an essential part of success. As the song goes, "They just pick themselves up, dust themselves off and start all over again." Because of this attitude, their worst day is often better than an average person's best day.

Sometimes we are our own worst enemy, taking our situations and ourselves way too seriously. Recently, I was reminded that it takes more than twice as many muscles to frown as it does to smile. We have to learn to relax and laugh a lot more, especially at ourselves.

Developing the ability to laugh at myself was a valuable lesson I learned after my speech course in Scotland. It proved to be a turning point in my speech recovery. When I returned from the course, the good news was that I wasn't stuttering anymore; the bad news was that I was speaking very, very slowly and in a very monotone voice—and louder than I normally would have. This was all part of the technique taught to me, and a temporary situation on the road to finding my new voice. From my perspective, I was fluent and I was willing to pay the price of this "minor" and temporary inconvenience. After a lifetime of stuttering and having people look at me strangely and dismiss me anyway, I decided that things were going to turn out just fine.

A lesson in laughing at yourself

On my way home from the speech course, I had to purchase my train ticket in Edinburgh, which, believe me, is a big deal to a person who stutters. I felt it was a good test to see what I could accomplish. I stepped up to the ticket office confidently, using my very pronounced speech technique and the exaggerated mannerisms I had learned. The ticket agent was a bit startled, to put it mildly, by the pace, tone and loudness of my speech, but to his credit (or mine) he gave me my ticket without asking me to repeat what I had said, or worse still, asking me to write it out on a piece of paper, which I had done many times in the past. As I picked up my ticket and turned to leave, feeling pretty good about myself and what I had accomplished, a young boy of about eight, who had been standing next to me with his mother, turned to me and said, "Mister, you talk funny." Children, as we all know, just say it like it is. His mum was embarrassed and told him to apologize to me, but I knew he meant no harm, and so told him it was okay and not to worry. As I was leaving, I looked at the boy and said, "If you think I speak funny now, you should have seen me before I got my problem fixed."

I left that ticket office with a smile on my face because I realized that for the first time in many years I had actually laughed at myself. I think in that moment, in my encounter with the young boy, I knew that everything was going to be okay—not easy, but okay. With that realization came almost a calm that I had not experienced before, and that was a true turning point in my own life.

Turning points do not have to be dramatic, they just have to be meaningful for you. The most important thing is to recognize them when they occur and use them to your advantage.

Reaching a turning point may mean that you have to learn to forgive others as well as yourself, and learn to let go of stuff you can't control and things that happened to you in the past. Yes, doing all this is sometimes hard, but you will be glad you did it.

Ask for Help

Asking, I believe, is the beginning of receiving. Some of the hardest words to say in the English language are: "I need your help." They are only four simple words, but the risk in them seems enormous. Some people, through ego, foolish pride, not wanting to look weak and vulnerable, or just wanting to do everything on their own, refuse to ask for help when they could benefit from it. The lesson I have learned is that the people who admit they have a problem or need help are not showing a sign of weakness or vulnerability. On the contrary, they are showing a sign of confidence and strength.

There is a saying, "We can do it, but we can't do it alone." For many years, I was one of those people who would not ask for help. Maybe I was fooling myself, but I thought I could control my stutter on my own. Asking for help and support was one of the most difficult but most rewarding decisions I could have made. It opened a whole new world of opportunity for me.

Surprisingly, whether it's on a personal or a professional level, most people do want to help others. Yes, there are always a few people who are not nice or who have issues of their own to deal with, but most people are good people, and it is human nature to want to help others, especially when asked.

Another useful way to use the "I need your help" phrase is when you are faced with a disagreement in point of view, or are involved in a dispute. If you step back, take a deep breath and let go of your position for a moment, asking for help to understand another's point of view will go miles in changing both your attitudes. You'll come to a mutually agreeable resolution a lot sooner.

"I need your help." They're four simple words, but very powerful ones, in business and in life.

Remember: A smart person can always win an argument and get in the last word, but a wise person knows how to avoid the argument in the first place.

Excellence is the result of caring more than others think is wise, risking more than others think is safe, dreaming more than others think is practical and expecting more than others think is possible.

—Successories Inc.

Seek to Be a Great Leader

People sometimes assume that great leadership is all about a role in business. How wrong they are. Leadership is about behavior, and not about fulfilling a role. Leadership is about action, attitude and vision, and leadership impacts all parts of our lives.

Leadership Is Not a Business Concept

When we talk of leadership, all too often we think of political or business leaders. One of the greatest challenges of true leadership today is raising and teaching our children.

Our children are in many ways an image of ourselves. Although we want to direct them, make them good people, and keep them safe, we have to let them grow up as individuals capable of making rational and thoughtful choices, especially since we cannot be there to monitor their actions 24 hours a day.

As you know by now, my wife Mary and I have two small children. We recognize that the tasks of teaching them right from wrong, setting an example for them, setting a high standard at home, and choosing the correct school system for them are our responsibility. As the 'leaders' of these small children, however, the only thing we can do is to be guides: to try hard to teach them to respect other people, to not take things for granted, to dream big, and to be well-mannered.

Leadership is about teaching your children right from wrong, teaching them good values and principles, and then living up to those values and principles yourself every day. Talk is cheap; it is your actions, the things you hold yourself responsible and accountable for, that get results. This leadership role is an ever-challenging responsibility, and I tip my hat to all the parents and schoolteachers out there, and especially to the single parents. Facing this responsibility on your own is an incredible feat of courage.

Leadership in business

In the business world, many people do not understand true leadership; rather, they attribute it to a role. For example, if you are the VP or the CEO, your leadership is assumed. Visionary leadership, bold leadership, spiritual leadership or courageous leadership is not about role, nor is it about giving orders or sitting behind some fancy desk. Truly great leadership is about knowing your people, understanding them, respecting them and nurturing them as individuals. Great leadership is being able to encourage and reinforce the level best of both individuals and teams.

> *Good leaders make people feel that they're at the very heart of things, not at the periphery. Everyone feels that he or she makes a difference to the success of the organization. When that happens people feel centered and that gives their work meaning.*
>
> —Warren Bennis, professor and author of
> 18 books, including *On Becoming a Leader*

Leadership is not about position, prestige or power. It is not something that can be given or taken away; it is earned by action. Good leaders know when to be tough, and when they have to make decisions that they know are not going to be popular, they make them with a compassionate heart. Good leaders treat people with respect. They are aware of the strengths and weaknesses of every team member and how to work with these traits in order to help each individual realize his or her true potential. They are able to talk to people on their own level and to understand their position on issues.

Today, people are seeking more than a paycheck. The organization that thinks it can buy loyalty through money is mistaken. In fact, I've interviewed hundreds of people and found that recognition, praise and involvement, as well as a having a trusted leader, were the key factors in deciding whether to stay at or leave an organization. Yes, they did look for fair pay and other incentives, but to earn their trust and loyalty, to have them stay with you, to have them feel empowered and to keep morale high, you also have to treat people well and engage their heart as well as their head and their hands.

People do work for money, but they work even more for meaning in their lives. In fact, they work to have fun. Companies that ignore this fact are essentially bribing their employees and will pay the price in a lack of loyalty and commitment.

—Jeffrey Pfeffer, author of
Six Dangerous Myths About Pay

Exercise: Signs of poor leadership

Take a look at the list below and check the behaviors that may apply to you:

At   At
work   home

[ ]   [ ]   Assuming that your role or title gives you the right to be called a leader

[ ]   [ ]   Managing by intimidation

[ ]   [ ]   Excluding people from discussions or decisions that will
               impact them

[ ]   [ ]   Having a 'closed door' approach

[ ]   [ ]   Saying you have an open door policy, but not living up to
               that invitation

[ ]   [ ]   Making 'your way' non-negotiable

[ ]   [ ]   Being inconsistent in decision-making or behavior

[ ]   [ ]   Setting a bad example

[ ]   [ ]   Sitting in the 'Ivory Tower' and being out of touch with
               your people

[ ]   [ ]   Not being open to hearing other's ideas or opinions

What is your action plan to adjust any behaviors you have checked above?

_____
_____
_____
_____
_____

Successful leaders make people feel respected and a part of their organization or family. Great leaders never stop listening or learning. Great leaders
let go of ego; they know it is not about them, it is not for them to take the
accolades and glory. They know it is about the people around them, be it
their employees, their children, or others. Never forget that rule. Always
make other people feel good about themselves.

Leadership is the ability to get ordinary people to do extraordinary things,
and to get them to do better every day. Leadership is the ability to maximize

each person's potential. Leadership is making people feel connected to something bigger than themselves, it is focusing on the possible, rather than the inevitable.

Ask yourself...

In what areas of my personal/at-home life do I feel I am a great leader?

In what areas of my professional/business life do I feel I am a great leader?

In what personal/at-home leadership areas would I like to improve?

In what professional/business leadership areas would I like to improve?

Take a long, hard look at your answers. Determine what you are doing well, acknowledge these areas and give yourself a pat on the back. Now, focus on the areas you need to improve, both in your personal and professional life, and then create and act on a plan for improving these areas.

Great leadership always starts from within, by recognizing your strengths, and also by recognizing your weak areas and being resolute about working on them.

Whatever leadership role you take on, be it parent, teacher, mentor, coach, business leader or manager—always think of leadership as a privilege, not a right.

Smart leaders create a corporate culture that unleashes, not stifles, human creativity.
                    —David Heenan, author of *Double Lives*

Find Balance

Never be so busy that you can't find the time for the
people in your life who are the most important to you.

Work/Life Balance

If we had the solution to the challenging problem of finding a work/life balance, wouldn't life be so much simpler! How to find this balance is something I am frequently asked about in my speaking business. Many people I come into contact with are very successful business people. They plan or have someone else meticulously plan their daily business life, but unfortunately they do a lousy job at planning their own personal life. Juggling your day so that you find enough time to be with the people you care about, and being disciplined enough to say "No" at times, are choices. Making thoughtful choices is a discipline that only you can practice for yourself, with a little help, of course, from those close to you.

There are sacrifices and compromises that have to be made in order to find our own work/life balance. The choices and decisions involved are sometimes not easy ones; in fact, they are frequently very tough.

Work/life balance is a serious business and should be treated as such. I'm amazed at people who do not see it that way. These same people wonder why their marriage or relationships with their children are breaking down, why they are getting sick at work, why they are stressed, why they do not seem to have any quality time to spare with the people they care about. For them, there are never enough hours in the day.

Work/life balance is not the same for everyone, nor is it about a nine-to-five workday.

Answer the following question honestly

On a scale of 1 to 10 (10 being high), how comfortable am I with my work/life balance?

If you gave yourself anything less than a 7, think about what it is that is stopping you from scoring higher. Think about what aspect(s) of your life you need to change in order to move your score up one notch. (Yes, this is something you must do one notch at a time.)

My wife and I both have busy careers. We both travel with our jobs and are very committed to serving our clients. With two small children at home who also have time commitments, it is easy for us to feel out of balance sometimes. In that regard, we are no different from many of you.

Once we had children, we sat down to discuss ways to maintain balance in our commitments to our professional work, to our family and to each other. We made a conscious decision to always be there for our children, to be home for important family occasions, and to sit down as a family for dinner as often as possible. To that end, we have made a concerted effort to travel only a certain number of days each month, and never at the same time. One of us is always home to put the children to bed at night. We also try to take one day on the weekend for family; no business work is done on that day.

In the past, I would bury myself in my office way too often, including on weekends. I would go into my home office and say I would be out soon, and then I would get involved in 'things.' Four hours later I would reappear. Now, however, the 'Closed' sign is on my office door on Saturdays and Sundays. We make it a point to schedule some all-important time for ourselves as a couple to go out for dinner or to a movie or to visit friends, and that means booking ahead with our babysitter. I also clearly mark off the days on my calendar when I need or want to be home (even though it is often tempting to forfeit the family day to take a paid engagement).

You work to live, not live to work.

—Mary Marcus, wife and mother

Living a balanced life takes meticulous planning and prioritizing. It takes asking some tough questions about what is truly, truly important to you and your family. How many hours do you want or need to spend at work? How many hours are you prepared to put toward commuting to and from work each day? Do you want to be home a certain number of nights each week to eat supper with your family? Do you really need to work through weekends? Do you want to be present at those important family occasions, especially when your children are young?

I can't answer those questions for you; only you can do that. But remember that good time management starts and ends with you. If you fail to manage your own life, other people will definitely manage it for you, and not always with your best interests in mind. The choice is yours alone, to make every day.

Your work is just your work; your life is your life.

—Sissey Spacek, actor

Honor Your Commitments

Successful people not only live up to the expectations they set for themselves, they also honor the commitments they make.

I know unforeseen circumstances can crop up, and sometimes we have to cancel out on things, but unless you have a genuinely valid reason for canceling, always do what you say you are going to do. That could mean keeping a dinner engagement with a work associate, going to a movie with your spouse or significant other, meeting a friend for a coffee or a drink, or watching your kids play an important soccer game. It could be something of major significance in your life or just a social occasion, but unless there is an emergency or something seriously unavoidable that comes up, keep your promises!

It is quite a revelation to discover the number of people who are genuinely surprised and honored when others make a commitment to them and actually stick to it. Being treated with such integrity always makes people feel special and important.

Find Time for Yourself

Do not feel guilty about time you spend alone. People are often embarrassed when they say they spent time alone, or "did nothing." Society, at least Western society, puts great value on creating quality relationships, a concept we have already discussed. What we do not value enough, though, is spending quality time alone, taking time to step back, think, plan or simply do nothing—by ourselves.

Give yourself that time and space. It is not selfish, it is enriching. Time alone can be time well spent and healthy. It helps us put life into perspective and thus creates more quality in our relationships with our loved ones.

For this time to be truly of value, it can't be taken haphazardly; you may even have to schedule it into your calendar. It is very important that the activity you spend this time on *not* be work-related. If you don't set aside non-work periods, you go into self-time starvation, and then when you do take time, it becomes repair rather than renewal time.

My wife finds renewal time very early in the morning. She will get up at 5 a.m., make coffee, get a book, and soak in the bathtub for over an hour. I, on the other hand, often find renewal time on a Sunday morning by watching the live English soccer games on TV, going for a jog, browsing in my favorite bookstore, or just taking a long walk in the countryside.

Action steps for spending some quality time alone

- Determine when you will feel best taking this time.

- Negotiate the time with your family.

- Think about the sorts of things you like to do on your own and schedule them into this time.

- Create the environment for renewal. Some individuals need complete silence; others need the stereo blaring or people around them.

- Schedule the time into your week and take it!

Make Time for Your Family

Equally as important as taking time for yourself is making time for your family and loved ones. All too often you hear about marriages in trouble and families breaking down because of lack of attention or quality time spent together.

Think of your life as a pie and divide it up into slices that represent all of your different roles: parent, spouse, worker, friend, individual, member of a sports team or hobby group. You need to allot time to each portion. As I said earlier though, time allocation cannot be haphazard. This is especially true for the portion that is spent with family.

You need to book special time with your family. This may appear to be a bit contrived, but trust me—and any workaholic around you will concur—if you don't make a point of scheduling it, then time for yourself and time for your family will be the first things to be sacrificed. Reserve one day each week for family. Book a date one night a week with your spouse or significant other. Make it something special that you both can look forward to.

Here are some ways you can use your family time:

- Take a mini-break every once in a while. Sometimes a whole week off is hard to get, but a long weekend is a bit easier. You can take a mini-trip to a city you have always wanted to visit, or you can book an overnight in a local hotel and pretend you are a tourist in your own city.

- Hire a babysitter and take your spouse or significant other out to dinner. (People with young kids can usually relate to this one in a big way.)

- Go visit an art gallery, museum or some location that is of interest to you.

- Take your children to a ball game or sports event. When my son Daniel was three, I took him to his first baseball game. We went to the Skydome in Toronto to watch our beloved Toronto Blue Jays. Okay, at three my son did not watch much of the game, but the whole experience, including the anticipation of going, taking the subway to the game downtown, sitting on the curb eating hot dogs and fries, buying our souvenir hats, and just being together, was a priceless one for a father and his son. It takes me back to when my dad took me to my first soccer game in Manchester when I was Daniel's age. The memory remains with me even today.

- Visit your local zoo, pack a picnic and find a nice park, or collect pebbles on a beach. Get out in the fresh air and away from technology for a while.

Exercise: Make time for yourself and your family

Below, list the people and groups you need to make time for. Decide how you are going to book time in your calendar, and then schedule the first date. Next, determine how you are going to use this time.

For example: My plan includes date nights with my wife, time for myself and time with my children, all planned to coincide with my wife's personal time.

Now create your plan:

Spend time with	Scheduled when?	Doing what?

While writing this book, initially I was working every evening and on weekends, and I was certainly not being fair to my family. Once I realized that I was being selfish and putting an unfair burden on my wife, I decided to make certain changes. I spent every evening with my family and then worked for three or four hours once the kids went to sleep. Or, I went to bed at a normal time and set my alarm for 4 a.m. so that I could work for a few hours before anyone else got up. On weekends I did the same so my kids would also see me. Was it easy? No, but it was the choice I had to make in order to accomplish my goals and live according to my values.

Successful people have the ability to make compromises and important choices in order to achieve goals and find balance. Their definition of success includes success at work, success in relationships, and success in life.

Do not overlook the importance of managing your life as well as your career. To manage one is admirable, but to be able to combine and balance both of them is the true essence of success.

Success Is a Journey

Have you ever noticed how many people are in such a hurry to get to their destination that they miss out on all the valuable lessons and beauty along the way? They don't realize that they can learn from both the pleasant and the tough experiences on the journey to success.

Mountaintops inspire leaders, but valleys mature them.

—J. Philip Everson

Success *is* a journey. With so many twists and turns, highs and lows, peaks and valleys, lessons to be learned, and battles to be won, why hurry? It is important to take time to reflect. We learn the really valuable lessons not so much through our victories, but from our defeats, our setbacks, and all the adversity we face. These are what build true character.

All the adversity I have had in my life, all the troubles and obstacles have strengthened me. You may not realize it when it happens, but a kick in the teeth may be the best thing for you.

—Walt Disney, visionary thinker and founder of the Disney Corporation

Success Is About Being Agile

Nobody can guarantee the future. Yes, you can have a clear vision of where you want to go and execute that vision by setting goals, making plans and acting on them; yet while such preparation will take you a long way, life isn't that simple. We have all, I am certain, experienced some potholes along the road and will continue to do so.

You can adhere to all the principles in this book, and I am honored if you do, but if you do not understand that life is a process that is constantly evolving, you will not achieve the success you desire.

Successful people recognize that achieving true success is not a spectator sport. They learn early to take the punches and setbacks that life throws at them and to bounce back. They are constantly making plays and taking time-outs to reflect on those plays and to strategize on the next play. Sometimes those plays are for defense and sometimes they are for offence. As long as you stay in the action and realize that success is largely a work in progress, success will happen for you—not always on your own terms, but in its own magical way.

Success Is About Making MAGIC

Magic does not happen on its own. Even a skillful magician has to practice his or her craft for years to perfect their performance. The MAGIC of success has guidelines:

M Be MEMORABLE. Always look for ways to stand out from the crowd.

A Have a great ATTITUDE. In the game of life and the game of success, attitude is everything.

G Be GRACIOUS. Treat others as you would like to be treated: be kind and thoughtful.

I Demonstrate INTEGRITY. Be true to yourself and to others: always do what is right and honest.

C Above all else, be COMMITTED. Figure out what you truly believe in and are truly seeking in life, and stay focused in that direction.

Success Is About Being Courageous

To be truly successful, you have to be courageous. To be courageous, you have to be able to ask yourself tough questions and answer them honestly.

Courageous questions

- What do I really want in life?

- What is truly my measure of success?

- Am I prepared to sacrifice what is necessary in pursuit of success?

- Can I say what needs to be said?

- Can I do what needs to be done?

- Can I make MAGIC?

Exercise: What courageous questions do you need to ask?

What questions do you need to *add* to the list?

_____

_____

_____

_____

_____

Professional courage

Courage applies to professional success as much as to personal success. The 'courage questions' in business are so important, yet many people are not willing to ask them. They may be afraid of rejection, or of what they might hear or learn. Having professional courage means being prepared to hear constructive criticism, and to learn from it.

Courageous business questions

The first step you need to take is to decide who will answer your courageous questions. Will it be your customers, your colleagues, employees, or possibly your boss?

As a salesperson, once I have answered my prospect's questions and concerns, and established that there is a fit between my offerings and their needs, I must be brave enough to ask the courage questions. The answers I receive will determine whether or not we have a future relationship or opportunity.

- Did you see value in the materials I sent you?

- Did the materials make sense to you?

- Do you have any other questions?

- Do you think what I offer would be a good fit for your company?

- Would you like to work together?

- How would you like to proceed? When would you like me to send you the contract to sign?

Exercise: Your courageous business questions

To whom do you need to direct your questions?

_____

What questions do you need the courage to ask?

_____
_____
_____
_____
_____

The wording of the questions is not crucial because each of us has our own style and way of doing business. However, the key to using the questions is that once you have overcome objections and established value, you must have the courage to ask for the sale/order/contract. I work with a lot of salespeople from many different industries who, to my amazement, do not ask for the sale. Do not be one of them.

THREE actions of highly successful people

1. They talk value, value, value.

2. They see everything from their prospect's point of view.

3. Once they have established that there is a fit between their prospect and themselves, they ask to do business with that person or company. They know when to ask for the order and how to CLOSE the sale.

Always think in terms of helping and serving your customers and clients, rather than trying to sell them something. Talk in terms of YOU and US instead of ME. That is the mindset and attitude of successful business people.

Success Is About Challenging Yourself Every Day

Successful people hang out with other successful people. They do not waste their time with those who are negative or envious. They seek out people who are forward thinking, ambitious, and able to push them to become better individuals. Other successful people do not intimidate them. On the contrary, they want to learn from those who are more successful than they are in business and in life.

Surround yourself with people who are going to motivate and inspire you. Author and motivational speaker Les Brown said, "If the people in your life can't bring you up, don't let them bring you down." That is an important message and one worth remembering.

Do one new thing every day. Stretch your comfort zone! Take a chance on something you have always wanted to try. The people who stand out from the crowd are the ones prepared to take that chance.

Challenge breeds success

I have a friend named Jim who, by his own admission, was an average tennis player. He played with a group of people who were at or near his level, and had a really good time, but Jim wanted to take his tennis game to a new level and to test himself. He knew he couldn't do that by always playing against the same people, so to challenge himself, he joined a new tennis club and started playing against people who were much better than he was. At first, he got beaten pretty badly, but his comments to me were that defeat spurred him on even more. The challenge to play at the level of these people encouraged him, even though he was losing all the time. It got his competitive juices flowing, and over time Jim's game improved tremendously. He learned so much more from losing against these stronger players than he ever would have done by playing and winning against those at his own level.

Eventually, and with lots of practice, Jim started to win every once in a while; and ultimately, he became much stronger and began to win more consistently. All of this happened only through playing with people who were better and stronger than he was, and by his pushing himself to the limit and getting out of his comfort zone.

Ask yourself...

• Where do I need to challenge myself?

• How can I find and connect with stronger players?

• Who can I learn from who can motivate and inspire me?

Principles on the subject of challenge

- Learn from the best constantly.

- Never begrudge investing in your personal and professional development.

- Take action now.

Success Is About Having the Right Role Model (or Coach)

When I first started my sales career, there was someone who motivated and inspired me, and his name was Harry Palmer. Harry was the top salesperson at one of the companies I worked for. He was a very gracious and wise individual, and I learned much from him.

When I joined the company, he gave me some sound advice that has held true even to this day. He told me not to keep company with people who were always complaining, who always had an excuse or blamed others for their lack of success.

Harry also encouraged me to attend sales seminars to learn my craft, to listen to tapes, to read business books, and to subscribe to our trade magazines. He told me to learn about my products and services, inside and out, so I could speak from experience and knowledge.

The others in our company made fun of Harry at our weekly sales meetings because during our breaks Harry was always busy making phone calls and writing thank-you notes while they were reading the newspaper and talking with each other. When they used to say sarcastically to Harry, "What are you doing now, writing love letters?" Harry's comment to me was, "While they choose to waste their time fooling around, I am making an investment with my customers, building a future for myself." His self-discipline is what took him to the top of that organization, and by providing me with an example, he contributed greatly to my sales success.

When it comes to choosing a mentor or role model, be prepared to learn from the best. Do not settle for anything less.

Exercise: Find a coach

What five people would you like to learn from or engage as a coach?

1. _____
2. _____
3. _____
4. _____
5. _____

Make contact with them; maybe ask them out for lunch.

Keep a Journal of Your Thoughts and the Wisdom of Others

One of the better decisions I made a few years ago was to keep a journal of my thoughts and observations. (I wish I would have done it sooner, but as my grandmother used to tell me, it's no use crying over spilt milk.) I do not use my journal as a diary to track my daily activities. I use it to capture my thoughts and observations about life, and for lessons I learn along the way. I also use it to capture other people's thoughts—maybe a quote I have seen or heard that resonated with me, maybe an article from a newspaper or magazine, something I read in a book or heard on a tape or something I learned at a seminar I attended. This journal has enriched my life in so many ways. It has given me tremendous wisdom and inspiration, and has provided wonderful material for me to use in my writing and presentations. It has been the source of many of the quotations I have used in this book.

There are no set rules for keeping a journal; I just randomly write in things as I discover them. The trick is to always carry a little notepad and pen or to keep your PDA (personal digital assistant) close at hand, so you can immediately note your thoughts. Otherwise, if you are like me, you will quickly lose that inspiration, maybe forever. I carry around a mini-recorder as well, so when I am driving and I think of something, I can just record it hands-free, with no danger to anyone.

I use my journals now as a resource, not just for professional and business purposes, but also to improve my personal growth or the well-being of my family.

A journal may or may not be the tool for you, but I do know of many successful people who use one. Try it out for 30 days or so, and see how it feels.

> *Knowledge is a process of piling up all the facts, and wisdom lies in their simplification.*
> —Martin Fischer

Success Is About Being Grateful

We live in a world of high technology, material wealth, and the expectation of instant results. What I feel has been lost to a degree are the simpler things in life, including a genuine caring about other people. In today's world, I think we take so much for granted.

I live in a fantastic country, Canada, which has one of the best standards of living in the world. Toronto (the city in which I live) has been voted by the United Nations as one of the most diverse and multicultural cities in the world; it is a place where the cultures truly do blend. Of course, we do have our problems—what country or city does not?— but what amazes me is that many people living here do not appreciate how fortunate they are. They complain and focus on the negative rather than being grateful for how blessed they are to be living in a free, open and democratic society. It is so much more useful to look at the bright side of any situation, and to appreciate what you have rather than what you don't have.

Take a moment to be grateful and appreciative of the life you have, but much more importantly, take a moment to be grateful and appreciative of other people who have helped get you there. It is just a little thing, but one that means so much to people. What does it cost to thank people? Show gratitude, speak gratitude and, most importantly, LIVE gratitude every day. It will give your life a higher purpose and meaning.

Success Is About Showing Respect

I judge people not just on how they interact with their peers, but also on how I see them behaving outside of a business setting, when perhaps their guard is down and they do not feel they have to make a good impression. The differences I see are often incredible. I watch how they interact in a restaurant and how they speak to the person serving them. You hear about this kind of thing all the time, about celebrities who are gracious and friendly when the cameras are rolling and yet are totally different, perhaps indifferent, even rude, when the cameras are gone.

Successful people send a clear message of who they are in the way they treat others and in whether or not they choose to show respect to people consistently.

A friend of mine, Cathleen, used to tell me that she judged the young men who wanted to date her daughter Sarah by how they behaved with their own mothers. Her reasoning was that if they treated their mothers with respect and kindness, it meant they would treat her daughter well.

Being respectful earns respect, and learning to be respectful starts at an early age at home. This book is about success, but for those of you who are parents, there is no greater success than seeing your children grow up to be outstanding citizens, to be young men and women who make you proud.

Success Is About Family and Friends

Truly successful people recognize the need to spend quality time with others. They take time for their family and friends. It is great to be materially successful, but not at the expense of those close to us.

I try hard to plan my calendar around my family. I take regular breaks and attend as many of my children's functions at school as I can. Our children grow up so fast, and my advice is that it is better to make less money and spend more time with the people who matter and for whom you care the most.

Ask yourself...

* How many times do I forget to say please and thank you to people close to me?

* Do I take other people for granted or do I acknowledge them?

* Do I take enough time to be with my children?

* How am I participating in the upbringing of my children?

Success Is About Living Your Values

Values are like fingerprints. Nobody's are the same but we leave them over everything we do.

—Elvis Presley

A lesson in values

In 1973, I went to work as a trainee hairdresser for the world famous Vidal Sassoon Company. I was just starting out, so I had all the 'special' jobs: washing hair, sweeping the floor, making the coffee.

One day we heard that Vidal Sassoon himself was coming to visit the salon. We were all so excited. Can you imagine?—here was a person who was a celebrity; he was in the media all over the world, and he was also our CEO. When the big day finally arrived and he came into the salon, he did something that taught me a lesson in values, respect and success that has stuck with me for years. Rather than going first to introduce himself to the senior stylists or to management, to our amazement, he went directly to the back of the salon to talk to us, the rookies, who washed the hair and swept the floors. He welcomed us to the business, to the art of hairdressing and to his organization.

This simple act taught me that no matter what you do in an organization, every person and every role is equally important. Vidal Sassoon demonstrated that everybody should be treated with the same respect and common courtesy, no matter what his or her title or position. He showed me the impact of making people feel special. I still remember my pride that day as he introduced himself: "Hi, I'm Vidal Sassoon, it's great to have you on our team. Thank you for your valuable contribution." He showed me what integrity truly is. He never forgot where he came from, where he had started out on his rise to fame.

FIVE Key Values of Successful People

Respect

Respect means treating people as equals, showing that they matter and that you value what they contribute to your life. Getting respect is a natural consequence, but to get respect, you have to earn it, and to earn respect you have to show it. Show people you really care about them and they will care about you.

Loyalty

In a world where people are sometimes fickle and superficial, I cannot stress enough the value of loyalty. Be loyal to the people in your life. Stand by them through thick and thin, in the bad times as well as the good.

Courtesy

Treat others as you would like to be treated: politely, kindly and with consideration. You can never be too courteous to people. Always be gracious and make people feel special and important.

Humility

Reputation is what people believe and say about you. Humility is keeping yourself grounded despite the success you may achieve.

Excellence

Excellence is not about destination; it is about action and focus. Even if your role is to wash hair, your goal is to be the best hair washer there ever was. Strive for excellence in everything you do.

Vidal Sassoon lived by these values. He cared about his people, and his people really cared about him. He treated all his employees with kindness and consideration. He was not only a person of tremendous success, but more importantly, he is to this day a person of tremendous significance.

A footnote to this story: A couple of years ago, when I was building a story about my experiences at Vidal Sassoon's, I decided to try and contact Mr. Sassoon personally to thank him for everything I learned at my time at his company. I tracked down where he still kept an office in Los Angeles and wrote him a letter explaining all the wonderful values and lessons I had learned from working for his company and how his visit to the salon all those years ago had left a mark on me. A week later I received a beautiful reply from Vidal Sassoon himself. I will cherish that letter forever.

Exercise: What are some of the lessons from Vidal Sassoon that can be related to your life?

_____

_____

_____

_____

_____

- Do you treat everybody you meet with respect?

- Do you take the time to recognize and appreciate the people in your life?

- Do you show gratitude to the people who have helped you along the way?

- Do you take the time to get to know new people you come into contact with?

Cross the Finish Line
on Your Own Terms

Success Is About Having No Regrets

We have all heard the expressions: "Life is so short" and "Life is for living," and, truly, it is. The cemeteries and graveyards are filled with people who didn't live up to their full potential, who had not done the things they had wanted to do. Unfortunately, it is too late for them, but it is not too late for you. Don't be a person who says, "I could have, I should have or I would have...BUT...!"

Sometimes we worry too much. We analyze every situation and think of a million reasons why we should not do something instead of being a person of decision, or a person who says, I CAN, I WILL! Success comes with action.

Success is not a spectator sport, and you get to choose every day if you want to be a player or whether you want to be a spectator and watch success go by.

Twenty-seven words to live by

Please	Thank you	Love
Risk	Believe	Listen
Observe	Desire	Commitment
Courage	Patience	Relax
Appreciate	Trust	Passion
Choice	Change	Respect
Care	Integrity	Faith
Compassion	Action	Understanding
Opportunity	Principles	Values

These are words I try to live by. Some may or may not be yours. Take a few minutes to put your own list together. Think about the words you choose and what they truly mean to you. Revisit them from time to time.

What words do you want to add or remove?

_____

_____

_____

_____

_____

Words are very powerful. Use them wisely, but heed the wisdom of Eleanor Roosevelt who said, "[Our] philosophy is not only expressed in words, it is expressed in the choices we make. In the long run, we shape our lives and we shape ourselves. The process never ends until we die. And the choices we make are ultimately our responsibility."

If you really want to do something, obviously within the law, do yourself a favor. As the Nike slogan says, "Just do it!" We are on this earth for such a short time. Have no regrets. When Sir Winston Churchill was asked, in the latter years of his life, what he regretted the most, he answered, "Spending so much time worrying about all the things that did not happen to me."

A lesson in no regrets

Rosalind was a successful lawyer living in a trendy waterfront condominium in downtown Toronto. She was popular, had lots of friends, a good income, all the trappings of a great life. But Rosalind was not happy. She had grown weary of her job. The long hours she had to work frustrated her and the money was not that important to her anymore.

What Rosalind really wanted to do was become an artist. It was her secret passion, one, she confided in me, she had been nurturing for years. Rosalind had to make a choice, but giving up the practice of law to become an artist was not an easy decision to make. Her parents had sacrificed much to put her through law school and she felt an obligation to them. She was unsure how her friends would react, but quite sure she would have to live a lot more modestly to pursue her passion to become an artist.

Ultimately, Rosalind did what was in her heart. She left her high-powered job and the big city to move to beautiful Nova Scotia on the east coast of Canada in order to pursue her dream. She now lives near the Atlantic Ocean in a modest cottage and shares a studio with other artists. It is a far cry from her former life, but Rosalind is successful on her own terms. She is totally happy with her life, and she is gaining some recognition as an artist. She agonized so much over her decision, but told me last time we spoke that she would have regretted it all her life if she had not followed her dream and passion. Rosalind is now living her version of success, and while it may not be yours, how many of us can say we are following our dream, our passion, and living life to the fullest—without regrets?

I know we have to be realistic, and we can't always do just what we want immediately, but I do believe that we can work toward a goal and we should never stop trying. The only limitations to achieving that goal are the ones we put on ourselves.

Too many people worry about what other people think of them. They are always trying to please others, just as Rosalind had for many years. They worry about what other people will think of their decision to want to do something different. Live your life for YOU because if you are not happy with yourself, if you don't respect and like yourself, you will not ultimately be able to give happiness and joy to the people who are near and dear to you.

Ask yourself...

- What do I want to do in my life right now? What need is it that I want to fulfill, and what will I regret if I don't do?

- What is holding me back from achieving my dreams?

- Am I settling for what other people want me to be and do, instead of fulfilling my life on my own terms?

- Is my image more important to me than my own happiness and state of mind?

Having no regrets is about taking that first step, being bold, going out on a limb, showing initiative and ingenuity, doing what you want to do and need to do. I have regretted many things in my life, including not taking that speech course years earlier. But, no more; what is done is done. Of course we can all learn from the past, but that should never stop us from doing something we want to do in the present or in the future.

My family and I have made a pact to visit Australia, and one day we will. We are planning for it by putting money aside every month. We look at maps to decide where we want to visit and for how long we want to be there. We are planting the seeds now, and by planning in advance, we are working toward our trip.

Confront your excuses for not doing what it is you want to do.

Exercise: Taking action

Write down three things that you really want to do:

1. _____

2. _____

3. _____

Now, start thinking about how you can be taking steps to move toward doing these things:

1. _____

_____

_____

2. _____

_____

_____

3. _____

_____

_____

Whether we are moving forward, taking a few steps backwards or just standing still, that clock is always ticking.

Success Is About Valuing and Using Time Well

When a defining moment comes along, either you define the moment or the moment defines you.

—Kevin Costner, actor

As I have mentioned before, time is truly our greatest commodity and most valuable asset. Since it waits for no one, it can also be our biggest opponent. "An ounce of gold," I once read, "will not buy an inch of time." How true!

How we spend those 86,400 seconds in a 24-hour period is our choice. We can either use the day wisely and productively, or we can go through the motions, wasting it or squandering it aimlessly, even letting other people tell us how to spend it. Time! Spend it wisely, otherwise other people will spend it for you.

A lesson in time

From the time I met her, Elizabeth, an old friend of mine in England, was always "sick." There were occasions when she really was sick, but most of the time it was all in her head. She seemed to take pleasure in telling her friends about all her ailments, all the medication she was taking, and listing all the misfortunes that had come her way.

Elizabeth rarely went out. She was a talented graphic designer, but she could not hold a steady job because of her imagined ailments. Whenever she did find work, she was soon fired for calling in sick too often. Her friends cared deeply for her and were fiercely loyal to her because she was a wonderful person when in the right frame of mind. She could be funny and witty, the life and soul of the party.

Her friends tried to help her, but to no avail. It saddened them to see such a great talent and wonderful person wasting her life with hypochondria. At the age of 38, however, Elizabeth had a major heart attack. Fortunately, she survived.

After her brush with death, Elizabeth was a changed person. That event had certainly been a wake-up call for her.

Once she felt stronger and the doctors gave her the all clear, Elizabeth moved out of the drab basement flat she had lived in for many years and found a nice roomy apartment in a high-rise building near a park. She started wearing bright clothes, had her long hair styled shorter, lost some weight, and started wearing makeup and jewelry. With her outlook on life and her personality changed, she was a more positive and happy person. She started dating and even landed a steady job, which she was able to keep. She took tremendous pride in herself, becoming the person she had really always wanted to be, like the Elizabeth we knew was deep inside.

What transformed Elizabeth? By her own admission, the near-death experience made her realize how precious and valuable time really is, and how in an instant it can be taken away. Her brush with death made her realize how much time she had wasted by "being sick."

If you are wasting your most precious commodity, TIME, don't wait for a near-death experience like Elizabeth's to reflect on life and change. Do it now, for all the right reasons.

Life is not measured by the number of breaths that we take, but by the moments that take our breaths away.
—George Carlin

Exercise: Managing your time

Five ways I can spend my time more productively and wisely:

1. _____
2. _____
3. _____
4. _____
5. _____

Success Is About Loving Relationships

Many people will walk in and out of your life, but a true friend will leave footprints in your heart.
—Author credit not known

As you can probably tell from my comments in this book, I am a happily committed family man with an incredibly supportive wife and two great kids. My family situation has taught me to cherish the people who are important to me in my own journey to success. Do not take your supporters for granted, but choose them wisely—there is nothing more important than having good people by your side, people who care about you in your personal or professional life. Successful people know the importance of having loyal people aligned with them.

I believe that the happier we are in our personal relationships, the more productive we will be in business. As much as we sometimes may try to hide our emotions and put aside personal troubles to act normally in our work environment, it takes a strong person to be able to switch their emotions off and on. The truth of the matter is that personal challenges do affect us by slowing us down and restricting our productiveness because our minds are not 100 percent focused on the task at hand. Likewise, what is happening at work follows us home at the end of the day.

While life is never completely free of conflict, the more open you are with your loved ones, the more quickly you can resolve disagreements. Your frankness and willingness to listen to each other pave the way to a loving relationship that is prepared for compromise despite the challenges.

Success Is About Leaving a Legacy

At the end of our lifetime, when it is time to switch off the lights and go upstairs to meet Our Maker, what will we be remembered for? It is not about the money we had in the bank or the possessions we owned; we can't take those things with us. What we will be remembered for, and the only things that will accompany us, will be our deeds. How many lives did we touch? How many people did we impact? What value did we provide people? What service did we deliver? What contribution did we make to society? Did we use our talents and creativity to the fullest? Were we kind to people along the way? Those are the questions we should be asking ourselves today because, ultimately, people will judge us by them. Leaving a legacy is all about deeds, value, service, contribution, kindness, talent, and touching people's lives in a positive way.

Many people today are obsessed with their mortality rather than their legacy. They preoccupy themselves with how long they are going to live. While this is not a bad thing, what is more important is to focus on the life represented by those years. Are you living every day to the fullest? Do you live life in the moment? We are just passing by this life on a journey. We should take each day as if it will be our last because one day it will be.

> Live your life so that when you die even the undertaker will be sorry.
>
> —Mark Twain

Ask yourself...

- What legacy do I want to leave?
- What do I want to be remembered for?
- Am I creating my legacy every day?
- Am I living in the moment?

Hold onto your dreams

No one can take your dreams away from you except YOU. Sometimes we are our own worst enemy; we do not believe we can achieve our dreams. My late colleague Art Berg said, "Dreams are made in the heart and mind, and only there can they be broken."

The Four Principles of Success

Remember the four principles of success that were described in Chapter 2?
Vision
Courage
Responsibility
Commitment

By maintaining a vision of success, and by holding onto the courage needed to achieve that vision through taking responsibility for your actions, and by adopting total true commitment, achieving success is only a matter of time.

We can all have the life we desire, the success we wish to achieve, but getting these will not just happen. Successful people are not spectators in life: they are active players, participants, visionary thinkers, risk takers, dreamers. They know what they want, and they are prepared to do what is necessary to achieve success.

Whatever point you are at on your journey, trust in the fact that you can make it—*if only you just hang in there.*

I challenge you to be bold and creative, to work hard, to be true to your principles, to respect people and build strong relationships. Do not forget to have integrity, show compassion and acknowledge the people who help you along the way. Keep in mind that the impossible is just the untried.

In Closing...

I am honored and privileged that you have taken the time to read this book, but what that shows me is that you are committed and serious about your success.

Success, my friends, is definitely not a spectator sport. It takes the brave, the bold, the resilient, the courageous, and the committed to succeed in the game. If you are prepared to do what most people will not do, the rewards are great.

I wish you great success on your evolving journey. Have patience, show flexibility, be true to yourself, and good things will happen to you. There is nothing, absolutely nothing, stopping you from having the success and life you deserve.

Have a great journey, and most of all, enjoy the ride along the way.

***When we have the courage to dream and the
commitment to succeed, a whole new world of
opportunities opens up for us.***

About the Author

Charles Marcus, originally from England, spent over 20 years in the sales and service industry, winning international awards for outstanding customer service and sales achievement. As a sales professional, he increased sales in his territory by 346 percent in one 18-month period. He later earned a leadership position with a major corporation and eventually moved on to become an award-winning entrepreneur. Today he runs his own successful professional speaking business.

What is truly remarkable about Charles's achievements is that for many years, Charles could not do what most of us take for granted—speak. For 25 years, he lived with a severe stuttering disability, suffering much ridicule, rejection and prejudice. He sometimes went for long periods not being able to speak at all, living in a world of virtual silence, and dreaming of one day speaking fluently in public.

Charles realized his dream after making an important decision: to take full responsibility for his life and to confront his challenges and fears head on. His powerful story of refusing to give up in the face of adversity, overcoming obstacles and winning against the odds has been featured in the international press and media.

Since 1999, Charles has been delivering customized motivational and inspirational keynote presentations and workshop programs on change, leadership, customer service, relationship selling and success to organizations all over the world. Some of his clients have included American Express, Canadian Tire Financial Services, Bank of Montreal, Clarica Insurance, T.D. Canada Trust, Freedom 55 Financial, International Association of Administrative Professionals, The North American Association of Asian Professionals, The Special Olympics, Prince Edward Island Teachers Federation and Sherwood Communications (U.K.).

Charles Marcus

International Keynote Speaker

Charles works with organizations that want to inspire their people to excellence by maximizing performance potential through building resilience, passion and pride.

Using illustrations from his own personal and professional experiences, Charles connects with his audiences in a way that empowers them to face the challenges and change in their own lives with renewed confidence and determination to succeed.

Charles is dedicated to working with you at your important convention, meeting or event, by tailoring an exciting and entertaining program that will not only motivate and inspire your people to action, but will also give them the tools, skills, strategies and mindset to make that commitment to excellence in their customer and team interactions—every single day.

Charles's message and presentation will leave lasting impressions and benefits for his audience long after the event is over.

Client comments

You took the time to understand the audience in order to ensure that your message hit home. A great speaker connects with his audience in a special way. You definitely achieved this.

—Marilyn Burjan, American Express

You clearly hit a home run, Charles, with our sales and service team. Thank you for your valuable contribution to making our event such a success.

—Michael Cooksey, Bank of Montreal

Even though there were fifteen hundred teachers present, you personalized your keynote to reach each participant. Comments from teachers identified your keynote as being "inspiring, honest, relevant and dynamic."

—Nancy Boucher
New Brunswick Teachers Association Elementary Council

You gave us tangible examples and ideas that our people, even our top sales performers, can apply to their client interactions right away. I have no doubt that your insights will generate real results within our organization.

—Sid Punjabi, Clarica Insurance

For more information on how Charles can work with you and your organization with one of his customized keynote presentations at your future event, please contact Charles personally at 416-490-6744 or at 1-800-837-0629 or via e-mail at charles@cmarcus.com. You can also visit his website at www.cmarcus.com

We Welcome Your Comments

If you have any comments on how this book has impacted your life, your organization, or both, or if you would like to share any success stories of your own, I want to hear from you. I will personally respond to every message you are kind enough to send to me.

Please contact me personally at:

E-mail: charles@cmarcus.com

Or, you can write to me at:

Charles Marcus

The Empowerment International Group

5863 Leslie Street

Suite 312

Toronto, Ontario M2H 1J8

Canada

Subscribe to Free Newsletter

The Empowerment International Group publishes a free newsletter via e-mail once every two months providing articles on personal and professional development, business success tips, quotes and recommended reading. To sign up for the newsletter, please visit www.cmarcus.com and click on the "Subscribe to Free Newsletter" link.

SUCCESS

is not a spectator sport

How to Take
Action and
Achieve More

Charles M. Marcus

Would you like to order copies of this book for your friends, family, employees, organization or customers?

To order, please contact:

The Empowerment International Group

Tel: (416) 490-6744

Fax: (416) 490-6344

Toll-free North America: 1-800-837-0629

info@cmarcus.com

you can also order directly from our secure website at

www.cmarcus.com

Please inquire about our attractive
discounts for orders of 10 or more copies.